The Yoga Sutras of Patanjali

A 21st Century Interpretation

Moises Aguilar

Edited By

Dan Mulvihill

To Carmen

Index

Introduction

Sutra: a rule or aphorism in Sanskrit literature.

The Yoga Sutras are a deep, enlightening, overwhelming and humbling book. After reading it twenty times you will still be learning from it. It is one of those books.

I started studying the sutras because I had to deliver them as part of the yoga teacher training program I co-teach with my wife. I have been reading philosophy my entire life so it was logical that I took care of this part of the training but the experience was bittersweet. The book had insight and really deep thoughts but every translation I found felt like pulling teeth. Very often the English translation was as obscure as the Sanskrit. The translators were using English words but when put together they did not make any sense. Some other times they did make sense and the ideas that came through were inspiring.

So I decided to write my own interpretation, one that could be fully read in English so I could use it as a teaching aid. I armed myself with seven different translations and started the work. I focused on the Sanskrit in the sutras. I studied their meaning and read as many commentaries as I could find. My goal was not to learn Sanskrit but to decipher the meaning of the sutras.

When reading great books one realizes that in essence they all explain the same things in a different way. Many topics in the sutras I had already read, mostly from J. Krishnamurti, whom I greatly admire. Ironically he did not have his own interpretation of the sutras but he analyses non-violence like nobody else and he asked, in my opinion, the ultimate philosophical question: "is there anything sacred beyond the mind?" Non violence (ahimsa) is one of the cornerstones of yoga and the question on the mind refers to purusha and prakriti in the yoga tradition. Both ideas are mentioned in the sutras.

During the writing of this book I had to go back to the beginning about five times. Every time a new concept became clear to me, it put covered areas into a new perspective. That required me to go back to the beginning and ensure that what had already been written was in line with this new realization. This will also happen when reading it. As you read it new concepts will click so when re-reading the book words will take new meanings and new realizations will become available. That is the trademark of a good book.

I made the English translation as approachable as I could while aiming at keeping the essence of the message. You will see the sutras flow as a continuous text which is not something I have seen translators do. Knowing Sanskrit is not enough to translate this book. One must understand the philosophical concept or the idea in the sutra will be missed. Understanding is the key word. You can only give what you have. This is my understanding of the sutras, nothing less and nothing more. As the Buddha said: don't believe a word I say.

Book 1: The Way to Samadhi (Samadhi Pada)

Interpretation of Book 1

(Sutra 1.1) Now, let's talk about yoga. (Sutra 1.2) Yoga is attained by removing the noise from the mind (Sutra 1.3) so you can remember who you are. (Sutra 1.4) Because when you forget who you are, you believe you are just a body living in this physical universe.

(1.5) Your beliefs can be subjective or objective. (1.6) Beliefs arise from five sources: correct knowledge, false knowledge, imagination, sleep and memory. (1.7) Correct knowledge can be obtained through perception, inference or through others; (1.8) false knowledge is perceiving something as different from what it is; (1.9) imagination is making things up; (1.10) sleep is a time when the mind rests, (1.11) and memory is recalling something that happened in the past.

(1.12) You can master and change your beliefs with practice and by not getting attached to them. (1.13) You will have to work on it for a while (1.14) until it becomes a habit, a way of life. (1.15) You should realize that you are not your beliefs and that you can change them. Do not become attached to them. (1.16) Realizing that this whole reality requires you to believe in it for you to experience it is called supreme detachment.

(1.17) You can remove your beliefs methodically, analytically, intuitively or via a realization. (1.18) Once these are removed, only pure information – reality – remains. (1.19) This is how things look when you are dead. (1.20) While alive, you must use wisdom, meditation, memory, resolution and faith. (1.21&22) The harder you work, the faster you get results

(1.23) Another approach is to look at life from the perspective of the universal consciousness. (1.24) The universal consciousness is beyond all that we can see. (1.25) Only from this perspective can you see how things really are. (1.26) This perspective is always available to the student, and it is the place where the true teacher lives.

(1.27) This perspective is represented by the word OM. (1.28) By repeating this sound you call this point of view to yourself. (1.29) When you repeat OM, your attention is turned inwards, which is where you can find this perspective, inside yourself.

(1.30) There are nine obstacles you can encounter that will prevent you from achieving this superior perspective. They are: physical illness, mental illness, doubt, a scattered mind, laziness, lack of self control, incorrect beliefs, failing to keep improving in your personal growth and failing to keep the superior perspective once attained. (1.31) You know you are suffering the consequences of one of these nine obstacles if you feel unhappy, depressed, restless or have difficulty breathing in a steady manner. (1.32) The best way to fight the nine obstacles is to meditate.

(1.33) When dealing with people, be nice to those who are nice, compassionate with those who are suffering, happy when meeting the wise and simply ignore mean people. (1.34) If you need to calm down, control your breathing (1.35) and focus on what you are doing to prevent the mind from wandering. (1.36) You can also focus your attention on someone you look up to who brings out the best in you. (1.37) Or just let go, chill out and relax.

(1.38) Paying attention to your dreams and the message they are trying to give you will also help. (1.39) Focusing on things or activities that you like will help as well. (1.40) By practicing these things you can learn to focus your mind on the very smallest to the most infinite of concepts.

(1.41) When your false beliefs are removed, the mind is like a transparent piece of glass. You can see things for what they are. Understand clearly what is in front of you. You cannot be fooled any more. You can see the true nature of things. (1.42) To gain this understanding you need to go beyond words. Words have preconceptions, assumptions and a history that affects what you see, so when you look at something and think of its name, your judgment is affected. (1.43) You also need to go beyond your memory or past experiences so they do not affect what you are looking at now. This would make you think that what you see is like what you have seen in the past and thus you would miss the truth of what is in front of you. (1.44) Words and memories affect your understanding of physical objects, concepts, ideas and beliefs alike.

(1.45) As the mind wandering becomes more and more rare, (1.46) you can tell you are on your way to samadhi(oneness), but not at samadhi yet. (1.47) With practice one gets better and better, (1.48) and can live life in the "truth", according with reality. (1.49) This experience – approach to life - is different than learning from others, or deducing what is going on based on what you can see. You are experiencing the truth. You can live firsthand what is really happening. (1.50) This knowledge - coming from interacting with reality - creates beliefs in you that prevent you from getting false ones. (1.51) When belief disappears, that pure state of mind where you find yourself flowing in reality in synch with what is, and connected to all that is, that is called samadhi, a state of oneness with all.

End of Interpretation of Book 1

Commentary to Book 1

(1.1) atha yoga anushasanam

(1.1) Now, let's talk about yoga.

The book starts with the word "now". This word implies that the student has prepared for this moment and some kind of prerequisite has been accomplished to get ready for this book. In India or Tibet they have gurus or masters. There the student trusts the guru to decide when the time has come to begin the study of philosophy. In the west it doesn't quite work that way. We like to make our own decisions, so having someone telling us whether we are ready or not is just not going to fly.

"Now" also means that we've had enough. We have searched and tried other things and have eventually grown tired of not finding anything that satisfied us. There comes a time in life when we want to find some meaning and going through the motions will not do anymore. This is also what "now" implies.

In the west we currently identify yoga with the physical exercise or asanas. As this sutra says, this book is about yoga so obviously there is more than asana. The western understanding of yoga, incomplete as it may be, is in line with our preference to make our own decisions. In the west, our understanding has to evolve along with our practice. As we practice more asanas – the physical part of yoga – our body and mind gets ready for more subtle truths. At some point we find ourselves ready to start delving into philosophy or breathing or meditation, which are all part of yoga. In the east one comes to yoga knowing that asana is just a part of it and one has to get ready for more, while in the west we come to yoga thinking that asana is all there is and then discovering that there is much more. The end result is the same, there are just two different paths.

My wife and I own a yoga studio in Chicago and we have seen students evolve in a certain way. Our experience is that when the student is ready, she will ask for more. It makes sense to us that asana is the first part of yoga we are introduced to. Even more so in the west. Yoga philosophy is not immediately obvious to the western background, so a gradual introduction works best. We also believe that we need to cleanse the body first so we can become aware of more subtle energies. The cleansing does not refer to juice fasting or diets, though healthier eating definitely helps. Cleansing refers to getting rid of stuck energies and stuff that we hold inside. Practicing asanas and making our bodies stronger, more flexible and agile will help remove these energy clogs, for lack of a better word.

In our studio we encourage people to come as often as possible. In less than three years many people have been there more than 250 times. As we had hoped, it was one of these students who approached us and asked if at the end of a class we could spend a couple of minutes in silence and meditating. This student had been able to flush enough stuff from the body so that more subtle practices started to be appealing to her. But as the western mindset demands, we had to give her the tools and let her get to that point by herself.

Someone who is totally new to yoga and is given the yoga sutras and is told that "this is real yoga", is probably going to run away, as she should. It is logical to start with asana. At first sight, it looks like gym class but more fun. And as the student keeps practicing, different internal experiences start to become available. Then, when the student is ready, she will ask for more. That "more" differs from person to person, but it is always something more subtle, more difficult to grasp.

Only after the student asks should the teacher bring up philosophy or breathing or meditation. If we try to play guru and decide that we know when someone is ready, we are bound to make one mistake after another. The teacher must present the tools and let the student use them. Forcing philosophy on a student because it is "real yoga" is not the way to approach yoga for our way of thinking.

Yoga is usually translated as union – also yoke or unite – but as there is so much more than that, I left the word yoga un-translated since it would be a disservice to yoga to think that it is just union. This entire book is about yoga as the first sutra says, so I'd rather let you read the book and make up your mind regarding what yoga really is.

(1.2) yogash chitta vritti nirodhah (1.3) tada drashtuh svarupe avasthanam

(1.2) Yoga is attained by removing the noise from the mind (1.3) so you can remember who you are.

The key word here is removing. Many sutras make this same point, that removing is more important than acquiring. The sutras explain how we are much more than we believe and the problems we have are the result of us forgetting, misinterpreting who we are, or just having too much going on inside our heads. All this prevents us from seeing things as they are. This sutra goes even further and it states that we can achieve yoga by silencing the mind and that remembering who we are is a consequence of yoga. Yoga is not the end goal but a tool that will enable us to find higher and deeper truths.

Removing the noise from the mind is a constant theme in the sutras. There are different levels of mind control but quieting the mind is essential in all of them. A mind that is all over the place is going to bring us unhappiness. According to the sutras, the main cause of our problems is having a mind full of noise, which would be in line with our current lifestyles. Since we first wake up and until we go to bed, we are bombarded with images, sounds and constant external stimuli. There is so much noise in our heads that it is hard to think straight. It is not so much how happy or unhappy our lives are, but how stable or fragile the setup is. How stable anything is in our lives is directly proportional to how strong our mind is. Only a strong mind will be able to get through the rough patches and enjoy the positive.

What we call "me time" is something that we like doing and helps us be more relaxed. "Me time" is an internal concept, something completely subjective. It is inside that we find the place to judge whether what we are doing is "me time" or not. And this is where the sutras say we can find ourselves, inside, once we quiet our minds.

The sutras go one step further than our concept of "me time" though. While we spend "me time" we don't really think about whom that "me" is. We just know that it feels good and recharges us. It nourishes some part of us that we call "me." This sutra states that if we quiet the mind, we will be able to remember and understand who we are. We'll get to that later in the book.

(1.4) vritti sarupyam itaratra

(1.4) Because when you forget who you are, you believe you are just a body living in this physical universe.

This physical experience is so intense that we think it real. We can see, hear, smell, taste and touch things. Our senses convince us this place is real. We can interact with the environment and the environment responds to our inputs. Is that not real?

The Indian tradition calls this physical universe "maya" – illusion. As quantum physics tells us these days we are not sure how volume happens since atoms are mostly space. These atoms when looked at really closely are 99% space. Then, somehow, magically, a piece of wood appears made out of atoms that are mostly space. The atoms are space, but the piece of wood is pretty real. Maybe there is something going on that we have not quite figured out yet.

The point of calling this place an illusion is not to dismiss it, but to take some of the pressure off. If all that we see is made up of space acting like solids, we could say that it is comparable to a computer game. We are the main character in the game, and the environment interacts with us. Just as the computer game has rules that make things seem to be there so we can interact with them, this reality seems to make things out of space so we can interact with them. We are born, the game starts, we live and the game plays out; and then we die and the game ends. We then come back and play another round. We get to experience joy, sadness, we make friends, have a family and learn things. If all this is actually an illusion, it is a pretty darn good one and it seems like someone made a really big effort to make all this up. Why dismiss it? Maybe it would be better to learn to enjoy it and get the most out of our experience.

(1.5) vrittayah pancatayah klishta aklishta

(1.5) Your beliefs can be subjective or objective.

None of the translations I have found use the word "belief" when translating this sutra. One of my assumptions when interpreting this book is that some words were just not available at the time the sutras were written. The author had to be creative and explain what a belief is using the words available at that time. At the same time, Tibetans have nine words for mind, so the opposite can occur as well and the English word may not exist for the Sanskrit concept. Throughout the book I try to use present-day words when possible but there are some words that I do not dare translate (like I did with "yoga") since using the western word would have missed too much of the meaning that the Sanskrit word had.

It is not so much that beliefs are subjective and objective. As Marcus Aurelius said, "Everything we hear is an opinion, not a fact. Everything we see is a perspective, not the truth." All beliefs are really subjective for they are ours. What happens is that some are correct, or come from correct perception, so they are objective; and the incorrect ones are subjective in the sense that they only exist in our heads.

(1.6) pramana viparyaya vikalpa nidra smritayah (1.7) pratyaksha anumana agamah pramanani (1.8) viparyayah mithya jnanam atad rupa pratistham (1.9) shabda jnana anupati vastu shunyah vikalpah (1.10) abhava pratyaya alambana vritti nidra (1.11) anubhuta vishaya asampramoshah smritih

(1.6) Beliefs arise from five sources: correct knowledge, false knowledge, imagination, sleep and memory. (1.7) Correct

knowledge can be obtained through perception, inference or through others; (1.8) false knowledge is perceiving something as different from what it is; (1.9) imagination is making things up; (1.10) sleep is a time when the mind rests; (1.11) and memory is recalling something that happened in the past.

Correct knowledge comes from others, inference or perception. As Will Rogers cleverly put it: "There are three kinds of men. The one that learns by reading. The few who learn by observation. The rest of them have to pee on the electric fence for themselves." If we follow Rogers' percentage distribution, we would say that one learns through others, the few learn by inference and the rest of them have to perceive the electric current traveling up to their bodies after peeing on the fence.

But that is the point, to have the experience. We so freely tag unpleasant as bad and pleasant as good. If we changed the measuring stick from pleasure to knowledge, our reading would also change. Actually, we already do this. How many times have we heard someone say: "that was the worst and the best thing that happened to me." It was the worst because it felt bad, but it was the best because we gained knowledge; knowledge about life or about ourselves. We all know that learning about life or about ourselves does have value regardless of culture, religion, nationality, race, gender or age. We also know that the best way to gain this knowledge is to experience it ourselves. The time comes when we truly want to pee on the fence, and we are very aware that it is electric.

(1.12) abhyasa vairagyabhyam tat nirodhah (1.13) tatra sthitau yatnah abhyasa (1.14) sah tu dirgha kala nairantaira satkara asevitah dridha bhumih (1.15) drista anushravika vishaya vitrishnasya vashikara sanjna vairagyam

(1.12) You can master and change your beliefs with practice and by not getting attached to them. (1.13) You will have to work on it for a while (1.14) until it becomes a habit, a way of life. (1.15) You should realize that you are not your beliefs and that you can change them. Do not become attached to them.

This is an important point. When it comes to defining ourselves, we recognize that the answer is complex. Still we all have something that we believe makes us who we are. It may be the place we were born, a group we belong to, our profession, a physical condition or the religion we profess. It gives us a sense of security, of identity. Not knowing who we are is an unsettling thought.

Beliefs are an important part of whom we have decided we are. These beliefs come along with the group that defines us, and challenging these beliefs is challenging the validity of the group, or the validity of our belonging to it. For each of us, there is a certain set of beliefs that cannot be touched. They are stored in the "do not go there" drawer. But those beliefs may be dependent on our circumstances. We need to differentiate between a true belief and a circumstantial one. These latter ones are there to validate the group and may hold no truth whatsoever.

As Krishnamurti explains, we should get rid of all our labels, all our circumstances and all our history. After removing all that, whatever remains is what we really are. And from that clean slate, we can build our beliefs back up. Build them without social standards, external impositions or human needs. Define a universe and a life that makes sense to us as human beings.

A belief system that is meaningful to us as human being must have both a universal and a local view. One compliments and corroborates the other. The universal view explains life as a whole and gives meaning to everyday life. The everyday view helps us with usual life situations and confirms universal principles. This system is more of a continuous process that evolves throughout our lives. Given our view of the universe and everyday life, we judge what is in front of us one way or another.

At a universal level we can see everyday life as a lesson or a punishment. If we see it as a lesson, we can compare it to a kid in school or to an explorer learning about a foreign environment. If we see it as an explorer, the environment can be foreign and dangerous or foreign and mysterious. We are choosing this perspective and with it we give context to our everyday experiences. This is our universal view, or what we think life is about. Given the universal view, we will see people either as teachers, opponents, brothers or aliens. Then we will behave according to our view of the people around us. The more constructive our perspective the more possibilities we will have. If we improve our belief system, I am not saying that we will like everyone, but the number of people that will annoy us will decrease. That I can guarantee.

(1.16) tat param purusha khyateh guna vaitrshnyam

(1.16) Realizing that this whole reality requires you to believe in it for you to experience it is called supreme detachment.

Supreme detachment goes beyond realizing that this reality is an illusion as we discussed in sutra 1.4. It adds that our belief in it is what holds the illusion together. Without our acceptance in the form of a belief, we would not be able to perceive reality the way we do. Our brains would not be able to decipher what we see, touch or hear. Our lives are not happening to us, we are allowing everything to happen around us. Not in a mystical way where there is a reason for everything and such. Our belief is helping make the translation of an atom being 99% space into a solid. That is how deeply involved in this reality we actually are.

(1.17) vitarka vichara ananda asmita rupa anugamat samprajnatah (1.18) virama pratyaya abhyasa purvah samskara shesha anyah (1.19) bhava pratyayah videha prakriti layanam (1.20) shraddha virya smriti samadhi prajna purvakah itaresham

(1.17) You can remove your beliefs methodically, analytically, intuitively or via a realization. (1.18) Once these are removed, only pure information – reality – remains. (1.19) This is how things look when you are dead. (1.20) While alive, you must use wisdom, meditation, memory, resolution and faith.

Of the three methods my favorite is the analytical way, although all of them play a part in the overall process. I am no mystic and have no visions on how the universe works. Things have to make sense for me. The universe is logical, cause and effect, action and reaction. Every process in the universe follows rules as logical as the laws of physics. That includes beliefs, ideas or any other psychological or mental process.

Special cases, exceptions, are gems for working though this process. These special scenarios are the entry point into a part of reality we have not yet considered. How should the universe work for this special situation to have its logical place in reality? If we can answer this question, we will find new rules and new information on how life works. Special scenarios are outside our box so every time we integrate a new scenario our box expands, making us wiser in the process.

It is not so much that we are enlarging our mental box, but that we are removing the restrictions that made the box small in the first place. Remember that in yoga it is about removing, not acquiring. Our natural view accounts for all scenarios, but we create a set of beliefs that restrict what we can accept. That is how the box is created. By removing the belief we dissolve the borders of the box and we accept reality.

(1.21) tivra samvega asannah (1.22) mridu madhya adhimatra tatah api visheshah

(1.21&22) The harder you work, the faster you get results.

We like to do what we do well. Stay in our comfort zone. Evolution, yoga, challenge, change and fun are all about getting us out of our comfort zone. But that requires an effort. This sutra is telling us that there is nothing we cannot accomplish if we work at it. And that the harder we work, the faster we will get results. It is a statement of human potential.

Working in order to achieve our goals is making it back to our culture. Sports companies or universities urge us to work hard and achieve our dreams. At the same time, our lifestyle is set up the opposite way. We buy the house, the car and the vacation and then we pay for it. Paying after the fact makes us focus on the mortgage rather than on the house, so we don't enjoy it so much. We value all the more things that have cost us effort to attain and we dismiss things that come easy to us.

(1.23) ishvara pranidhana va (1.24) klesha karma vipaka ashayaih aparamristah purusha-vishesha ishvara (1.25) tatra niratishayam sarvajna bijam (1.26) purvesham api guruh kalena anavachchhedat

(1.23) Another approach is to look at life from the perspective of the universal consciousness. (1.24) The universal consciousness is beyond all that we can see. (1.25) Only from this perspective can you see how things really are. (1.26) This perspective is always available to the student, and it is the place where the true teacher lives.

There are two important concepts introduced in these four sutras. The first is "ishvara-pranidhana", which is usually translated as surrendering to a higher power, and it is mentioned later as one of the practices to follow. In the context of this sutra, we are surrendering our point of view and look at reality from a higher perspective. The key is to give up, to truly consider, even for a moment, that we are wrong and try another point of view. In this case, a point of view which is more universal. And here is where the second concept comes in, purusha.

Imagine that everything, the entire universe, other possible universes, the past, present and future, all space and time that has been or will be; everything with capital "E". All caps actually: EVERYTHING. Imagine all that. The ALL, again with all caps. Now, imagine that this ALL is in someone's head. The owner of this head that holds ALL is conscious. Conscious of itself and conscious that there is a universe going on here. The consciousness of the one holding everything in its head we call purusha. Purusha is not this being beyond everything. Purusha is the consciousness of this being. This being is beyond everything we can know and all we can come in contact with is its consciousness. This consciousness we call purusha. Purusha is a universal consciousness, aware of everything, playing a part in everything. But it is just that: consciousness. It does not have matter, mind, body, nothing. Just consciousness. Overall universal consciousness.

So taking the perspective of the universal consciousness is looking at life from the perspective of the one who holds reality together, the one that imbues everything with life and is aware of everything. Everything we see in the universe is there thanks to purusha. So the good, the bad and the ugly, they are all there because of purusha. This is the universal consciousness point of view that the sutra tells us to consider. If we could look at reality from this point of view, we would understand what we see.

From the perspective of purusha there is neither good nor bad. Purusha is behind everything, so everything is its creation. Everything is as holy or as insignificant as everything else since all comes from the same place. No being is above any other being from the point of view of purusha. Both the mightiest of gods and the lowest of ants have the same dependency and relationship with purusha. Life looks quite different from there.

(1.27) tasya vachakah pranavah (1.28) tat japah tat artha bhavanam (1.29) tatah pratyak chetana adhigamah api antaraya abhavash cha

(1.27) This perspective is represented by the word OM. (1.28) By repeating this sound you call this point of view to yourself. (1.29) When you repeat OM, your attention is turned inwards, which is where you can find this perspective, inside yourself.

There is a beautiful explanation of OM in the Mandukya Upanishad. OM comes from AUM. The "A" is our physical reality; the "U" is the dreaming world or the subtle energies; the "M" is the causal or mental world; and there is a fourth and last part which is the silence after singing the word which represents consciousness itself. Singing this word helps us turn our awareness inwards, where we can tap into the purusha perspective.

(1.30) vyadhi styana samshaya pramada alasya avirati bhranti-darshana alabdhabhumikatva anavasthitatva chitta vikshepa te antarayah

(1.30) There are nine obstacles you can encounter that will prevent you from achieving this superior perspective. They are: physical illness, mental illness, doubt, a scattered mind, laziness, lack of self control, incorrect beliefs, failing to keep improving in your personal growth and failing to keep the superior perspective once attained.

It seems rather cruel to identify physical illness as one of the obstacles to achieving a superior perspective. That is only if we believe curing illnesses to be out of our league, which we mostly do. This is why we think it is so cruel. If we thought that we can cure ourselves, we would not think it to be cruel. If the sutras said that to attain the purusha perspective we needed to shave our heads, we would be ok with it since we can shave them. Since the sutras identify physical illness as an obstacle, maybe what they are saying is that we can do something about it. The same applies to mental illness.

Doubt, the next obstacle, applies mostly to our uncertainty regarding our ability to attain the purusha perspective. Doubting that we can become enlightened. Since this is one of the obstacles that we can remove, the sutras are saying that we can achieve enlightenment. That everybody can.

If a scattered mind is one of the obstacles, we need to throw the television set out the window right now. We are surrounded by things, people and companies that are continuously asking for our attention, scattering our minds in the process. There is a lot going on these days, which make life more fun. However, some dedicated and peaceful time is also a good idea once in a while. A scattered mind is like a bucket full of holes which is unable to keep water inside. The holes are each of the things that we are giving our attention to.

I'll skip laziness and lack of self control for obvious reasons, as well as incorrect beliefs since they are discussed at more depth in other sutras.

The next obstacle refers to a universal truth that we usually enunciate as "if it's not going up, it is going down." Nothing can be stationary, everything is moving. If we are not on our way up, getting a bit closer to enlightenment, we are on our way down, getting away from it. There is zero chance that we are going to stay in the same place for too long.

The last obstacle is related to the previous one. Once we achieve the superior perspective, we need to keep working to maintain it. If we stop moving up, we are going down, therefore losing this superior perspective. Think about the number one team in the league. That team is there because they work to stay there. The same applies to the purusha perspective. Unless we continuously cultivate it, we can lose it. This means that we can achieve this perspective during our lives. This is not something to enjoy elsewhere or once we are dead, but something we can attain and keep while alive.

(1.31) duhkha daurmanasya angam-ejayatva shvasa prashvasah vikshepa sahabhuva

(1.31) You know you are suffering the consequences of one of these nine obstacles if you feel unhappy, depressed, restless or have difficulty breathing in a steady manner.

(1.32) tat pratisedha artham eka tattva abhyasah

(1.32) The best way to fight the nine obstacles is to meditate

According to the sutras, anything we need to fix we can fix with meditation. So, let's consider for a moment that this is actually true. This implies that if we have a physical illness, since that is one of the nine obstacles, we can meditate and cure ourselves. This obviously makes no sense. But the reason it makes no sense is that we are looking at the problem from the perspective of our western belief system. Let's consider a different belief system, a more Oriental one maybe.

We have a body, we are not a body. Since our body is a separate entity from ourselves, it exists as its own self. We get to use it during our lifetime and when the time comes, we die and let it go. The body goes back to the Earth where it came from – ashes to ashes – and we go on our own way. This body we are borrowing during this lifetime is attached to us, linked to us, but it is not us. It is a body.

Second, let's entertain the notion that everything in the universe is conscious. The source of everything is consciousness (purusha), so something not being conscious is just not an option. However, not everything can express its consciousness as well as we can. Actually we can express our consciousness because we have a body that helps us to do so. The body is not expressing itself, it is expressing us.

So our body is a conscious individual entity. This means that we can communicate with it. And we can communicate with it via meditation. Through meditation we can connect with our bodies and find the answers to why we are having physical illnesses. If this sutra is true, and we can fix the nine obstacles with meditation, all the obstacles are therefore psychological in nature.

The body is helping us deal with this place. It is reacting to our belief system and protecting us as best it can from the rawness of this reality. Through meditation we can learn the reasons why our body has developed the illness that afflicts us. The reason for the illness will always be a false belief. When we replace the false belief with a correct one, the illness can go away as its job is done.

We take for granted that a correct belief is constructive, positive and uplifting, which we intuitively know to be the case. The fact that reality is so positive says a lot about the universe we are living in. Also, if the reality of the universe is so positive, it also implies that all the problems we are having today are self created and that they can go away. They are artificial, as in created by us. We are doing something to keep painful situations alive. Unless we did, the artificial and painful situation would not be able to exist by itself.

It is not our wrongs that hurts us the most, but those things we think we are doing well. Keeping a bad habit that we think is a good idea is the expression of a false belief in action. And this is why changing our belief system is so hard, because we think we are doing the right thing. The nine obstacles are not punishments, they are clues. Clues giving us a hint of how life and our heads really work.

(1.33) maitri karuna mudita upekshanam sukha duhka punya apunya vishayanam bhavanatah chitta prasadanam

(1.33) When dealing with people, be nice to those who are nice, compassionate with those who are suffering, happy when meeting the wise and simply ignore mean people.

Think about relationships from a point of view of giving and taking energy from each other. If someone is nice and gives us energy, then we should give back. If someone is suffering and needs energy, we should give them our attention and therefore our energy. If someone is wise, we should be happy and exchange is not necessary. And finally, if someone is nasty and wants to steal our energy, we should ignore them so they cannot take it from us. No attention, no energy lost. What mean people want is our energy. The way they get it is by playing on our flaws and thus capturing our attention.

Of these four cases, the most interesting is obviously the one involving nasty people. Why can this guy push my buttons? If we had no buttons to push, nobody would be able to push them, obviously. One way to develop these buttons is during our childhood. The button is an interaction or a situation that triggers a psychological protection mechanism. Wilhelm Reich describes this process in his book The Function of the Orgasm. During childhood we develop these programs to protect ourselves from pain. The purpose of the program is to get us through the painful situation with the least suffering possible. Unfortunately, while the program gets us through the tough time we lose consciousness to some extent. With the loss of consciousness comes a loss of energy which makes us feel depleted, which is just how we feel after going through a bad time.

The first step to get rid of these programs is to realize that we are no longer the child that had to develop them. Second is to watch the process of the program as it unfolds. When we find ourselves going through a difficult situation, we just need to watch and stay conscious. After watching ourselves enough times, we will be able to take control, thereby removing the program.

(1.34) prachchhardana vidharanabhyam va pranayama (1.35) vishayavati va pravritti utpanna manasah sthiti nibandhani (1.36) vishoka va jyotishmati

(1.34) If you need to calm down, control your breathing (1.35) and focus on what you are doing to prevent the mind from wandering. (1.36) You can also focus your attention on someone you look up to who brings out the best in you.

Don't we do this already? When someone is freaking out we tell them to breathe so they calm down. In the movies, after the cop has lost his partner, he focuses on the job to keep the mind away from the loss and the pain. And when we want to perform well at something, we invoke the champion inside of us. These three tricks have made it already to western culture.

In the yoga tradition it is said that the mind and the breath are like two fish that swim together. By controlling one of the them, the other follows. The mind is said to be more slippery so it is recommended to focus on controlling our breaths first. By controlling the breath, the mind follows.

(1.37) vita raga vishayam va chittam

(1.37) Or just let go, chill out and relax.

Some people may have a problem with my interpretation of this sutra but look at who were the first ones to practice yoga here in the west: hippies! Letting go, riding the wave or living in the now are very much eastern philosophical concepts. The west likes black and white while the east likes grey. The west likes to make plans and have goals, and the east prefers to live the now.

Have you noticed how in the latest superhero movies the good guy has some dark side and the bad guy has some light? In Indian culture not all the gods are that nice. They all play an essential part in the universe but some of them wear a necklace of human skulls. The Indian gods reflect the complexity of life and its moral dilemmas. In the Bhagavad Gita, Arjuna is torn with the moral dilemma of going into battle against people that he respects and Krishna convinces him that killing them is the appropriate thing to do. In the east, life is presented as a complicated ethical dilemma that we need to navigate through. This is what we are seeing in the superhero movies now. Since the nineteen forties Superman did everything right and the bad guy was totally evil but that is no longer the case.

Letting go is also in line with "ishvara-pranidhana" – surrendering to a higher purpose. Let go of our own life not by just ignoring it, giving up, or dismissing it, but by surrendering to a higher power, a higher purpose. This view seems to offer less control over our lives and we obviously don't like that in the west. We like to make our own decisions and feel that we have control. However, we do not have control over everything. It is at these times of upheaval when we can resort to this surrender and accept what is happening to us as a necessary experience to help us grow.

(1.38) svapna nidra jnana alambanam va (1.39) yatha abhimata dhyanat va

(1.38) Paying attention to your dreams and the message they are trying to give you will also help. (1.39) Focusing on things or activities that you like will help as well.

(1.40) parma-anu parama-mahattva antah asya vashikarah

(1.40) By practicing these things you can learn to focus your mind on the very smallest to the most infinite of concepts.

This exercise strengthens the mind. The same way we can exercise our eyes by alternating our sight between a close and a far point, we can exercise our minds by alternating our focus between something very small and something very large. Something small would be a particular topic or a concise problem. Something large would be the purpose of life, the structure of the universe or how complex social systems evolve.

The mind is the main driver in deciding what we do for a living. It's how we plan our professional life or how we recruit employees. Therefore people that are detail oriented should perform one job while big picture people should perform another. The more mind, the higher the position. The more detailed the mind, the more detailed the position. The more scattered the mind, the more scattered the job prospects.

The Native American Elder was giving a speech to corporate executives. He explained to them how he saw corporations depleting the planet of resources. To that, an executive responded that he understood what he was saying, but that he could not stop. As executive, he had a responsibility to his stock holders that he had to fulfill. To that, the Elder asked the executive if he had children. He said yes. Did he have grandchildren? He said yes as well. So the Elder asked, when do you cease to be a CEO and become a grandfather? The room became silent. That question was something our mind based corporate paradigm could not answer.

The mind is a wonderful thing that allowed us to have the engineering, medicine and technology we today enjoy. But the mind is a tool, a tool at our service. The mind has no perspective unless we bring that perspective in.

(1.41) kshinna-vritti abhijatasya iva maneh grahitri grahana grahyeshu tat-stha tat-anjanata samapattih

(1.41) When your false beliefs are removed, the mind is like a transparent piece of glass. You can see things for what they are. Understand clearly what is in front of you. You cannot be fooled any more. You can see the true nature of things.

"We have met the enemy and he is us" as Pogo said. If our minds were clear of anything that distorted our vision, we would be able to see things as they are. We would know how to treat everybody in every situation, what everyone's role in our life was, what the things in front of us were really worth, or what to spend our time on. If we could answer these questions perfectly, whom could we blame but ourselves if we didn't have the exact life we wanted? So, who is responsible then for not being able to answer them?

We blame others because we doubt ourselves. We think there are things out of reach, when they are actually not. As mentioned before, the sutras have a very uplifting view of the human being. They always urge us to get rid of our wrong perceptions, not to gain new ones. Our natural perception is already correct. And that is quite an optimistic message.

(1.42) tatra shabda artha jnana vikalpah sankirna savitarka samapattih (1.43) smriti pari-shuddhau svarupa-shunya iva artha-matra nirbhasa nirvitarka (1.44) etaya eva savichara nirvichara cha sukshma-vishaya vyakhyata

(1.42) To gain this understanding you need to go beyond words. Words have preconceptions, assumptions and a history that affects what you see, so when you look at something and think of its name, your judgment is affected. (1.43) You also need to go beyond your

memory or past experiences so they do not affect what you are looking at now. This would make you think that what you see is like what you have seen in the past and thus you would miss the truth of what is in front of you. (1.44) Words and memories affect your understanding of physical objects, concepts, ideas and beliefs alike.

(1.45) sukshma vishayatvam cha alinga paryavasanam (1.46) tah eva sabijah samadhih

(1.45) As the mind wandering becomes more and more rare, (1.46) you can tell you are on your way to samadhi(oneness), but not at samadhi yet.

Samadhi is an internal state of being, a perspective, something that occurs inside of us. It will express outward in our everyday lives, but any outside expression is a consequence of the internal state. Our minds being stable is a requirement to achieve samadhi but it is not samadhi. The stability of our minds is a measure of how we are doing. It measures our understanding of life, the universe and ourselves, how much control we have acquired and our ability to skillfully interact with our environment. We do not need any special situation to have a stable mind. We actually want to develop a stable mind regardless of the situation.

(1.47) nirvichara vaisharadye adhyatma prasadah (1.48) ritambhara tatra prajna

(1.47) With practice one gets better and better, (1.48) and can live life in the "truth", according with reality.

With this stability of the mind comes an understanding of how life and the universe work. The same way, with a better understanding of life and the universe, it becomes easy to stabilize our minds. This is a process, not something that we acquire spontaneously. Even if it comes in a flash, it does come due to all the work done prior to that moment. We have to work on it to get results, just like with any other skill.

(1.49) shruta anumana prajnabhyam anya-vishaya vishesha-arthatvat

(1.49) This experience – approach to life - is different than learning from others, or deducing what is going on based on what you can see. You are experiencing the truth. You can live firsthand what is really happening.

There are two ways of changing or advancing: the first is evolution, the second is transformation. Evolution has an established path that the student goes through. Each stage of the path requires certain conditions to be met in order to pass to the next stage. The evolution path is represented by what we call "the system." This system offers us a life path that when followed hopefully provides us with a good life. The system offers structure and predictability. Everybody starts here.

The second path, transformation, is based on firsthand experience. There is no structure or predictability so it is not for everyone. Some people are thrown to this path when their life situation cannot be handled by the system; others look for this path when the system is not enough anymore; and in times of change, when the entire mindset of the people living in the system evolves as a whole, the current system is abandoned and a big adjustment happens. The system transforms by integrating methods and information found through the transformation path and redesigning new evolution paths according to a higher understanding.

This is a natural centralization/decentralization process that human systems go through. Meaningful transformations of the system have already occurred in history. For example, how the system adapted to women's rights or religious freedom. Before people were able to choose their religious beliefs, they had to agree with the beliefs of the country they lived in. They had the option of evolving through that system, or looking elsewhere for firsthand experiences and self transformation.

The way to samadhi is pure transformation. No system can give it to us. A perfect system would take us all the way to the final stage, so we just take one last step by ourselves into samadhi. That system would provide us with a path to evolve until we acquire a correct understanding of the universe and life, as well as the skills necessary to develop a stable mind. Although our system is not there yet, it is open enough to provide us with avenues to look for this. If we think about it, that is not a bad system.

(1.50) tajjah samskarah anya samskara paribandhi

(1.50) This knowledge - coming from interacting with reality - creates beliefs in you that prevent you from getting false ones.

As we experience reality firsthand we develop our own theory or philosophy of the universe and life. Since these beliefs come from our experience, they are really strong. Having no doubts about them, prevents incorrect beliefs from creeping in.

(1.51) tasya api nirodhe sarva nirodhat nirbijah samadhih

(1.51) When belief disappears, that pure state of mind where you find yourself flowing in reality in synch with what is, and connected to all that is, that is called samadhi, a state of oneness with all.

As correct as these final beliefs are, they are still an interface to reality. Everything must go if we want to connect, merge, become one with what is in front of us. We can connect at an individual level or at a universal level. Both views are available to us.

Once we are able to connect we can see the true nature of things. There is no mental process any more as said is sutra 1.2 – Yoga is attained by removing the noise from the mind. There is total acceptance of what is in front of us and we can see it with a universal point of view – ishvara pranidhana. There is a feeling of bliss and all the obstacles (sutra 1.30) are removed, even for an instant, both from our minds and bodies.

We humans long for connection. We long to be seen, heard and touched. We want to be truly seen, truly heard and truly touched. We want others to see who we really are, to understand what we are truly saying and to be touched with meaning, in a way that is significant to us.

We need to merge with ALL if we want to merge with all of its parts. This is not instantaneous but a process(sutra 1.47). Most of us already have something we can connect with. We are able to experience samadhi with it. As our understanding increases we see how everything else is just as pure and we can connect to it as well. We realize that the reason we cannot connect to something is inside of us, and that once we change our perspective the doors open and connection is possible.

Notice how this sutra does not say that we merge with the ALL and disappear. Remember how one of the nine obstacles is failing to keep the superior perspective once attained. We are supposed to enjoy samadhi in our lives. Samadhi is our natural state of being.

End of the Commentaries to Book 1

Book 2: The External Practices (Sadhana Pada)

Interpretation of Book 2

(2.1) You need discipline, persistence, self study and surrendering to a higher purpose in order to realize the fruits of yoga. This is yoga in action. (2.2) These practices do not get you samadhi, but they help to put you in a position where samadhi can be achieved.

(2.3) There are five causes of suffering: ignorance, lack of empathy, the need for self-affirmation, clinging to the physical body and fear of change. (2.4) Of these, ignorance is the root cause of all the others.

(2.5) You believe you are your body and that physical life is all there is. (2.6) You also identify yourself with your human mind and you think that things are just how you perceive them through your senses. (2.7) Identified with body and mind, you like what feels good, (2.8) and dislike what feels bad; (2.9) and self preservation is the main driver of your actions, even for the wise.

(2.10) But the reasons you like or dislike something are beyond the body, so you must look into more subtle causes if you want to get rid of suffering. (2.11) Meditating and pondering about them will help you find these reasons. (2.12) Your current beliefs, whether correct or incorrect, are the result of your past, whether from this or past lives, (2.13) and as long as you have incorrect beliefs you will keep incarnating.

(2.14) While going through life, you reap what you sow. (2.15) To the wise, everything is potentially painful, whether by having it or losing it as everything in this life is transient. (2.16) But you can avoid future pain. (2.17) In order to overcome pain, you must not identify with your body or mind as these are temporary. It's the attachment to temporary things that brings unhappiness. (2.18) These temporary things are not random but follow, or are the result of, a definitive purpose. That purpose, and therefore the goal of these temporary things and everyday life is to teach you and help you understand the universe you live in. (2.19) Throughout life you will find new, recurring, special or about to occur situations.

(2.20) If you want to see the true nature of things, you must look without judgment. (2.21) The purpose of those things is to reveal their true nature to you (2.22) and pain ceases once you see it. You will still be affected by your environment or the actions of others since life goes on, but you will be able to handle situations more easily. (2.23) You will be drawn to those situations that will help you understand yourself (2.24) since not knowing yourself is the cause for you being here. (2.25) Once you understand yourself, life loses interest since its purpose is fulfilled.

(2.26) To understand yourself use continuous, discriminating analysis. (2.27) Following the first seven limbs of yoga, you can obtain this wisdom (2.28) as they clean up the impurities that do not let you see yourself as you are.

(2.29) The eight limbs of yoga are: yama (don't do this), niyama (do this), asana (yoga postures), pranayama (regulation of the breath), pratyahara (withdrawal from the senses), dharana (concentration), dhyana (meditation) and samadhi (oneness).

(2.30) The five yamas are: don't harm, don't lie, don't steal, don't lust, don't covet. (2.31) These yamas become a great vow when applied universally, to everything, all the time, and in any situation. (2.32) The five niyamas are: be clean, be thankful, be committed, be introspective and be trusting of a higher purpose. (2.33) Don't let the wrong mindset prevent you from practicing the yamas and niyamas. If that is the case, turn your mindset around to help you achieve them. (2.34) The wrong mindset may make you hurt others; arises from greed, hate or stupidity; can be mild, moderate or acute, but it always brings sorrow. This is why one must always cultivate the right mindset.

(2.35) When you are deeply rooted in not harming others, your mere presence brings peace. (2.36) When making decisions based on reality, your course of action is guaranteed to be the most appropriate. (2.37) When you stop wanting material things, more valuable jewels become available to you. (2.38) When you flow with the rhythm of life your life becomes effortless. (2.39) When you follow a simple life, you will be able to find your true purpose. (2.40) When you cleanse your body of toxins, emotional and physical, you will want to preserve this state of cleanliness (2.41) and with this cleanliness comes the ability to focus the mind, see the truth, control the senses and gain self realization. (2.42) When you are thankful for the things in your life, you will be happy. (2.43) When you are dedicated and determined, you become master of your own body, taking control over it instead of being controlled by it. (2.44) When you study yourself, you can understand how the universe works. (2.45) When you know yourself, you become one with the universe.

(2.46) Yoga postures (asanas) should be practiced by holding them for some time until they feel comfortable. (2.47) They should be practiced without expectation but focused so the mind is empty. (2.48) Through practice comes freedom from duality.

(2.49) Observing and controlling the inhaling and exhaling of the breath during the asana is called pranayama. (2.50) You can make your breath longer and more subtle by varying the three aspects of breathing: inhalation, exhalation or retention. You can vary the length, how many times you do each, or the area of the body you are focusing on. (2.51) There is a fourth aspect to breathing, a more subtle one, in which you gather prana not through the nostrils but at an energetic level. (2.52) Through this last aspect of pranayama, your false beliefs can dissolve and disappear. (2.53) Through these pranayama practices, the mind gets trained to focus and concentrate.

(2.54) When you focus and concentrate internally so much that you forget you have a body, as if the senses were on pause, that is called pratyahara. (2.55) Then you can have control over how you relate to the world.

End of Interpretation of Book 2

Commentary to Book 2

(2.1) tapah svadhyaya ishvara-pranidhana kriya-yogah

(2.1) You need discipline, persistence, self study and surrendering to a higher purpose in order to realize the fruits of yoga. This is yoga in action.

Yoga is a way of life, a philosophy of life, an approach to life. Just like the Tao provides a universal approach to life, so does yoga. Although it comes from India, it is not necessarily attached to the Indian religion. Trying to give yoga religious connotations is unnecessary. The yoga sutras do not have the ceremonial, devotional or structural sides that religion adds. It is a philosophy and we can use it as such.

Persistence, self study and following a higher cause are not foreign concepts for us. The temple of Apollo at Delphi displays the maxim "Know Thyself", and the concept of making sacrifices for a greater cause is used nowadays in team sports. As we apply this advice to our lives we want to combine these three practices into a single approach.

Surrendering to a higher purpose or cause is comparable to understanding life as happening through us more than to us or by us. We are playing a part in the universal game and we play this part as a willing participant, contributing our piece. We need to voluntarily surrender, so it is in our hands whether we want to participate or not.

Surrendering is actually not as easy as it seems. Surrendering is not letting ourselves be used as puppets, but making our actions be in harmony with universal perspective. Surrendering requires making enlightened decisions. Playing this role well in the universal game depends on how well we know ourselves. If we are driven by a set of wrong beliefs we will probably not make the decisions that would keep us in line with any universal goal. Only from the point of view of the universal consciousness can we be expected to make universally sound decisions. Therefore, surrendering and knowing ourselves go hand in hand. Surrendering will help us understand ourselves and knowing ourselves will allow us to surrender properly.

Finally, persistence is the attitude that must surround everything we do. Persistence requires working hard but more importantly not giving up. We must keep going. Not giving up will allow us to differentiate between persistence and stubbornness. Stubbornness will get us to a point and we will hit a wall. Persistence will help us to take two steps back and go around it.

Of the three, persistence is the most important. Persistence is what connects us to the ground, what keeps us connected to reality. Surrendering is the most subtle, self knowledge is the way to surrendering, and persistence is the way to self knowledge. As profound as yoga concepts can be, the sutras always remind us to keep our feet on the ground. It is the simple things that work. Those basic things that help us stay connected with reality.

(2.2) samadhi bhavana arthah klesha tanu karanarthah cha

(2.2) These practices do not get you samadhi, but they help to put you in a position where samadhi can be achieved.

Samadhi is a state of being. It is not something that comes from outside but something we achieve through an internal transformation. No practice can give us samadhi. They can help us to get to a place where the transformation is possible, but the last step is ours. The practices can get us to the door, but we need to walk through it.

(2.3) avidya asmita raga dvesha abhinivesha pancha klesha (2.4) avidya kshetram uttaresham prasupta tanu vicchinna udaranam

(2.3) There are five causes of suffering: ignorance, lack of empathy, the need for self-affirmation, clinging to the physical body and fear of change. (2.4) Of these, ignorance is the root cause of all the others.

If we try to find a common theme to these five causes, the theme is me, me, me, me, me. Maybe that is not by chance. If this reality is an illusion (maya) and our real self is somewhere closer to a universal consciousness (purusha), coming here for the first time must be quite a shock. When we are living in this physical reality, we do so as individual entities. Since purusha is universal and we have an individual entity, somewhere somehow the process from universality to individualization has to occur. Maybe this process occurs through what we call suffering. Maybe suffering is just the first phase we all have to go through during our first lives in this physical universe. Then, as we learn to deal with this place better, we learn to live, we do not need to focus so much on ourselves. Suffering may just be how becoming acquainted with physical reality feels in the beginning.

Think about how it was when we were learning to drive a car. Dealing with the pedals and the lines on the pavement was enough in the beginning. Our driving was totally selfish. There was no empathy whatsoever towards the needs of other drivers. Our car was the only safe place in a road full of things moving around. How scary was it just to change lanes.

Ignorance was reflected in not knowing how to drive. Lack of empathy on not being able to care for anybody else on the road since driving our car was already hard enough. The need for self affirmation was expressed as our need to own the lane, to make others respect us on the road. Clinging to our physical body was reflected on deeming being inside our car as the only safe place on the road. And fear of change was shown in something as simple as switching lanes.

All these causes of suffering sound like the mistakes that someone would make when faced with something for the first time. Maybe that's all there is to it. We all of us go through these kinds of suffering when we come here in the beginning.

(2.5) antiya ashuchi duhkha anatmasu nitya shuchi sukha atman khyatih avidya (2.6) drig darshana shaktyoh ekatmata iva asmita (2.7) sukha anushayi ragah (2.8) dukha anushayi dvesha (2.9) sva-rasa-vahi vidushah api tatha rudhah abhiniveshah

(2.5) You believe you are your body and that physical life is all there is. (2.6) You also identify yourself with your human mind and you think that things are just how you perceive them through your senses. (2.7) Identified with body and mind, you like what feels good, (2.8) and dislike what feels bad; (2.9) and self preservation is the main driver of your actions, even for the wise.

(2.10) te pratipasava heyah sukshmah (2.11) dhyana heyah tat vrittayah

(2.10) But the reasons you like or dislike something are beyond the body, so you must look into more subtle causes if you want to get rid of suffering. (2.11) Meditating and pondering about them will help you find these reasons.

(2.12) klesha-mula karma-ashaya drishta adrishta janma vedaniyah (2.13) sati mule tat vipakah jati ayus bhogah

(2.12) Your current beliefs, whether correct or incorrect, are the result of your past, whether from this or past lives, (2.13) and as long as you have incorrect beliefs you will keep incarnating.

Being forced to re-incarnate sounds like a punishment but it only does because we think about the tough times in our lives. How about the wonderful things in life? If we had enough of these, wouldn't incarnating be the greatest thing?

Happiness and enjoyment are the clue that we are figuring things out. Initially we are thrown into a new environment and it takes us a while to learn how to deal with it. Once we learn how to live, life becomes enjoyable. The better we know how to play the game, the more we enjoy it.

As long as we have incorrect beliefs, correct ideas will look wrong to us. The right perspective will be alien until we align with reality. In the beginning everything will seem an effort and tough. The funny thing is that the effort never goes away, we just learn to enjoy it. We start to appreciate the process and all the knowledge it provides through what we now call pain. Once we learn to enjoy it, there is no longer any pain. Think about a thrill ride in an amusement park. The thrill is part of the enjoyment. The same happens with life. The uncertainty, the change, the good and bad are all parts of the ride and once we learn to enjoy the process it all becomes as fun as an amusement park.

Actually the amusement park is a good analogy. We get in the ride and have the experience. After the ride, we can discuss it and let the experience sink in. After a while we become bored again and ready to get on another ride and the process repeats. This process of experience, realization, stagnation and back to experience is a natural flow. The more of these cycles we can go through in life, the more intense our lives become. The more intense, the more realizations we come to and the more alignment with reality is possible, thereby breaking the incarnating cycle.

(2.14) te hlada-paritapa-phalah punya apunya hetutvat

(2.14) While going through life, you reap what you sow.

What makes us sow what we sow? Could we have sown anything else than we did? Are our lives already as good as they could be? We immediately think that of course they could be better. We could be rich and famous, or have found our soul mate and live happily ever after. But then we would have to deal with being rich and famous, or know how to be happy ever after with our soul mate. If someone made us rich and famous, how do we know we can stay that way by ourselves? If we find our soul mate before we know how to have a relationship, how long do we think it is going to last?

Skills are more important than things, even if the thing is a soul mate. Only the right skills will guarantee that we can keep something once acquired. Also, only if we have the right skills will we know what to do when the opportunity arises.

When it comes to skills, would you rather have one amazing skill but nothing else, or would you rather be good at many things but not outstanding at any? The answer is we want both, and we must work towards acquiring both. Think of a piano player who has amazing technique but is not so good choosing the pieces to play in the concert and it is very hard to work with when playing with an orchestra. Now think about a piano player who is not as good technically but knows how to choose pieces that will please the audience and is very personable so orchestras like to work with him. The second one with a more balanced set of skills will probably do better in the long run. However, those that were best had all. They were fantastic players, knew how to choose the right pieces to play and could work with others.

Our issues or shortcomings usually define us more than our assets. Although we should improve ourselves – after all, we are our own most important work – we want to stay true to ourselves. It is not so much about changing who we are but figuring out how to do the best with what we have. The point is to discover our natural abilities and to work on them; to also realize our shortcomings and minimize their negative effect in our lives. We must learn to deal with ourselves, to learn how to get the best from us. That is a life fully lived. One where we have understood ourselves and have figured out how to best fit into our environment. Each one of us would implement the solution differently since we are all unique, but each one of us would have created a unique piece of art: our own lives. A natural ability that is not cultivated is like a rough diamond left in the mud. A neglected area in ourselves is like a patch in front of our eyes that does not let us see.

The other side of the coin is opportunity. We can prepare ourselves as much as we want but we still need the opportunity to appear. In order to create opportunities for ourselves from scratch we would need a lot of skill, lots of effort and some luck. Ideally the environment should be capable of providing opportunities. Our current environment comes from society and the economy. To be able to work on our passions we must be able to make a living out of it since we still have to pay the rent every month. It is our job to figure out how to put our skills to best use given our environment.

(2.15) parinama tapa samskara duhkhaih guna vrittih virodhat cha duhkham eva sarvam vivekinah (2.16) heyam duhkham anagatam (2.17) drashtri drishyayoh samyogah heya hetuh

(2.15) To the wise, everything is potentially painful, whether by having it or losing it as everything in this life is transient. (2.16) But you can avoid future pain. (2.17) In order to overcome pain, you must not identify with your body or mind as these are temporary. It's the attachment to temporary things that brings unhappiness.

This sutra is usually translated as "life is suffering" but we will get into that later. What is irrefutable is that everything is potentially painful. This is the dark side of the yin-yang. Even the most wonderful thing in the world has a dark side. The most beautiful relationship would bring us pain if it was to end, and as we gain knowledge we lose innocence.

From this perspective there are two approaches to life. The first approach is cold, in which we do not become too attached to anything. We do enjoy things to some extent but we stay safely detached. The second one is hot, in which we jump in with two feet and get attached to what is in front of us. We fully enjoy what we do but suffer when it is gone.

If we take the cold approach, we can stay cold to most things but sooner or later we need to commit to something. We need a fully engaged relationship. These relationships are the ones that give the most meaning to our lives. At the same time we cannot fully engage with everything. If we give ourselves fully to the first thing that comes across, when we do find something worth connecting with we will be out of gas. When we fully connect with something we will probably suffer, but it will be something worth suffering for.

(2.18) prakasha kriya sthiti shilam bhuta indriya atmakam bhoga apavarga artham drishyam (2.19) vishesha avishesha linga-matra alingani guna parvani

(2.18) These temporary things are not random but follow, or are the result of, a definitive purpose. That purpose, and therefore the goal of these temporary things and everyday life is to teach you and help you understand the universe you live in. (2.19) Throughout life you will find new, recurring, special or about to occur situations.

As unfair as life may seem at times, it is never false. Physical reality may be an illusion but the rules that drive it are real. Learning how to live life better will help us understand the universe since the rules that rule the universe also rule this physical reality. "As above, so below" says the Kybalion, or in more modern terms, we live in a holographic universe.

Using everyday life as a tool to understand deeper spiritual truths is a powerful resource. When we say that something is spiritual we just mean that it has to do with other dimensions of ourselves (souls or spirits) and that its scope is broader. Simply put, the study of humans in the context of Earth is anthropology, while the study of humans in the context of the universe is spirituality. All we did was enlarge the scope from Earth to the universe.

In our pursuit of knowledge, we should work from the bottom up, from the physical to the spiritual. We sometimes make the mistake of taking spiritual thoughts for granted, and trying to make sense of them in everyday lives. Unless we can prove a statement in everyday life and physical reality, it remains a theory. Once the theory becomes practice, then we can call it truth. All this time, we've had the most powerful resource of information in the universe, our own lives. Spirituality should be a consequence of our understanding of how the physical plane works, not the other way around.

Spirituality must be built from the ground up and it is the physical reality which teaches us how the spiritual reality is. We don't need anything but our own power of deduction, intuition, and our ability to think to come up with spiritual truths. Let's compare the lifecycle of the body, which we understand well, with the lifecycle of the spirit, which we know nothing of. The body is born, grows, matures and dies. Pretty simple. If we live in a holographic universe, the spirit must follow the same lifecycle. Somewhere the spirit is born, then it grows, matures and should die. Although this sounds strange to the western tradition, it is not alien to the Hindu religion. In Hinduism, the universe follows a cycle of creation and destruction and everything appears and disappears in a day of Brahma. Just as we have days and nights, the universe has the same in the Hindu religion. During the Day of Brahma the universe is created and destroyed, and during the night it is dormant, waiting for the next day to start.

(2.20) drashta drishi matrah suddhah api pratyaya anupashyah (2.21) tad-artha eva drishyasya atma (2.22) krita-artham prati nashtam api anashtam tat anya sadharanatvat

(2.20) If you want to see the true nature of things, you must look without judgment. (2.21) The purpose of those things is to reveal their true nature to you (2.22) and pain ceases once you see it. You will still be affected by your environment or the actions of others

since life goes on, but you will be able to handle situations more easily.

How do we find something that we don't know is there? We can only find it with an open mind. If we have a preconception of what we will find, we will compare the outcome to our expectation and the answer will only be, "yes, that is what I expected", or "no, that's wrong." That is how we mostly think. We construct a world in our heads in order to be comfortable, to deal with life, and we like this world to change the least possible. Every time it changes, we have to make an effort to readjust so we try to avoid anything that will question our construct.

The only way to look at the world with non-judgmental eyes is to feel safe, and in order to feel safe we need to know we can deal with change. Change is inevitable since the reality we are in is an illusion and we have a drive towards reality. Our false preconceptions and false beliefs will fail progressively and a real appreciation of the universe will be realized. The only constant in this process is change. Therefore, our ability to deal with change is an essential skill to acquire in life.

By embracing and enjoying change we get rid of preconceptions and we are able to look at the world with new eyes all the time. Then we can find something new. The only way to find the unexpected is not to have expectations. And to not have expectations all we have to do is expect change since change is grounded in reality.

Pain ceases once we look at it differently as discussed in sutra 2.12. It does not go away, it is just seen differently, as providing information or as something exhilarating. Our lives do not need to change for us to feel better. Our understanding of our lives does though. It is this understanding that makes the difference and allows the good side of life to be enjoyed.

(2.23) sva svami saktyoh svarupa upalabdhi hetuh samyogah (2.24) tasya hetuh avidya (2.25) tat abhavat samyogah abhavah hanam tat drishi kaivalyam

(2.23) You will be drawn to those situations that will help you understand yourself (2.24) since not knowing yourself is the cause for you being here. (2.25) Once you understand yourself, life loses interest since its purpose is fulfilled.

We humans are curious creatures and that could serve us well in this situation. These sutras suggest that the events in our lives are not random at all, and that the decisions we make are not random either. We gravitate towards the situations we require in order to understand ourselves. Situations are giving us clues about who we are and how we function.

If this is the case, our current situation in life is a message. Life is trying to tell us something. The purpose of this message is to help us understand ourselves. What we need to do is stop and think about why our lives are the way they are and what that means. Most of us only think about our lives when we face some kind of unfortunate event.

We need to get into trouble in order to think about anything meaningful. While things are well, we follow other people's lives on television. Nothing in our lives is coincidental. At any point in time the best and worst parts in our lives can help us understand ourselves. The goal of our lives is neither to make us suffer nor to entertain us, but to give us information. This is happening all the time, not just in times of trouble. However, trouble is the signal we need to follow to think about ourselves. The troubles we face provide the most information about what we are missing. If we understood ourselves and we understood life, we would not be suffering.

Then, once life fulfills its purpose and we understand ourselves, we will lose interest in it. It is the difficulties, the suffering, the unknowns, the surprise and the unexpected that keeps us interested in life. It is our ignorance that makes life appealing. If we knew everything we would be bored.

(2.26) viveka khyatih aviplava hana upayah (2.27) tasya saptadha pranta bhumih prajna (2.28) yoga anga anusthanad ashuddhi kshaye jnana diptih a viveka khyateh

(2.26) To understand yourself use continuous, discriminating analysis. (2.27) Following the first seven limbs of yoga you can obtain this wisdom (2.28) as they clean up the impurities that do not let you see yourself as you are.

We can analyze and study our lives all the time. Why do we look the way we do, or have the job we have, or the relationships we have, or the hobbies we have? All these are not by chance. We gravitated toward all of them to live situations that would give us information about ourselves. The sutras do not tell us to use intuition or meditation to understand ourselves but analysis. We can decipher our lives in a logical manner, following an analytical process.

The first seven limbs of yoga that are listed in the following sutra will help us with this analysis. They will help us remove the misconceptions that do not let us see ourselves properly. The eighth and last limb is samadhi itself.

(2.29) yama niyama asana pranayama pratyahara dharana dhyana samadhi ashtau angani

(2.29) The eight limbs of yoga are: yama (don't do this), niyama (do this), asana (yoga postures), pranayama (regulation of the breath), pratyahara (withdrawal from the senses), dharana (concentration), dhyana (meditation) and samadhi (oneness).

The eight limbs are sorted in increasing levels of complexity and subtlety. Also, the limbs build on top of each other. The first limb is a list of things to stop doing followed by a list of practices to follow. Then we engage the body through asana and the breathing through pranayama. After working on the breath we take control of the senses by actually disengaging them all into a state of pratyahara, which connects us with the mind. The mind leads to concentration, deep concentration leads to meditation, and meditation to samadhi.

We cannot ignore the first practices and expect to get much out of the subsequent ones. The limbs can be worked simultaneously but must eventually be completed in order. If we are having trouble with a yama, we shouldn't focus on concentration just because it sounds cooler. The missing yama will prevent us from realizing the benefits of concentration.

At the same time, the limbs should be worked on cyclically. Once we are following the yamas and we start working on the next limbs, our understanding of the yamas will evolve and we will need to readjust to meet the yamas once again. The important part is to try not to cheat. We would only be cheating ourselves.

Working on any limb will also help us with the others. To some extent, all the limbs are progressing in parallel. Not understanding one will prevent us from realizing the others, but working on one will help us advance in general. The limbs help us to understand life and our understanding of life will determine our understanding of the limbs. Understanding is understanding and it applies to everything, yoga and its limbs or life and its situations.

(2.30) ahimsa satya asteya brahmacharya aparigraha yama (2.31) jati desha kala samaya anavachchhinnah sarva-bhaumah maha-vratam

(2.30) The five yamas are: don't harm, don't lie, don't steal, don't lust, don't covet. (2.31) These yamas become a great vow when applied universally, to everything, all the time, and in any situation.

A particularity of the yamas is that they are associated with a third party. Don't harm others, don't lie to others or don't steal from others. The goal of the yamas is to start making us conscious of what we do and the consequences of our acts. Also, the goal is to make us realize that there are people around us that we affect with our actions.

Ahimsa, don't harm or non violence, is one of the core principles of yoga. The principle of ahimsa is intimately related to accepting everything around us. As Krishnamurti explains, putting labels on anything is already an act of violence because it brings separation. Even when we say "I am a man" we are separating men from women which is a violent act. Our human nature draws us towards judgment as long as we believe we are a body. We are born either male or female, we have a certain race, nationality and language. All these aspects of ourselves are labels that we acquire as we live our lives. The principle of ahimsa is asking us to transcend the physical view we have of ourselves. We exist beyond the body. That is where our true self resides. This true self cannot be described with the labels we use for our bodies. That is also what the act of violence refers to. By using labels on ourselves we are identifying with something we are not. We exist beyond our body and anything that says the opposite is an act of violence.

Another area of violence we deal with every day is language. It is not only the derogatory terms that exist in every language but the implicit meaning behind the words. Look at the terms "fat" and "heavy set". We think that saying "fat" is impolite and insensitive and the appropriate term is "heavy set". The only reason we cannot say "fat" is because we have implicitly judged "fat" as being wrong. That is why we think we need to use another term. So every time we say "heavy set" what we are really saying is that we deem fat to be a bad thing. Instead of accepting everyone as fat or thin, we create labels that are appropriate or inappropriate. This is also an act of violence.

Krishnamurti goes even further in saying that anything that creates duality is an act of violence. Even saying "I am non violent" is an act of violence because it is implicitly labeling something else as violent. Non violence requires the acceptance of everything as equal and the removal of all judgment. We need to call things as they are and accept them as we see them. We all know how to do this, we all did this when we were children. Children have not yet been "educated" to use words in a certain way therefore they are honest. Kids playing in the park do not care about the gender, race or nationality of the kid playing with them. They don't care either about how fat any of their game companions are. The education process we all go through is what creates the prejudices and our need for labeling.

As we pursue non violence we must go back to one of the principles of the sutras, the process of undoing. Our path does not consist so much in acquiring new things but in removing. In this case we need to remove the effects of the education we received and re-learn to use our natural abilities to look at the world. Our labeling comes from fear and the fear from believing we are a body, as sutra 1.3 states. Once we understand we are much more than our bodies, getting rid of judgment becomes possible.

Of all yamas, the most important one for our personal development is "don't lie." We should never lie to ourselves about anything. How we look in others eyes or what others think of us is meaningless, only our opinion counts. We should be as aware as possible of our intentions in everything we do, as our intention is what will allow us to follow the yamas. The difference between resting or wasting our energies is in the intention we have while laying down. The difference between coveting or having goals is also in the intention. Clean intentions will help us to easily follow the yamas so we must be totally honest to ourselves about them.

A second aspect of not lying is the pursuit of truth, the pursuit of reality. This aspect is fundamental in yoga and it is what makes life meaningful. The pursuit of reality is a perspective we must consciously take. If we go on a pilgrimage and all we do is walk down the road looking at the scenery we just went on a long walk. What makes the experience a pilgrimage is the internal meaning we apply to the experience. The pilgrimage is an internal experience. It is our perspective that made it such. The same way, the pursuit of reality is an internal process. Reality is inside of us. Not lying requires us not to focus on the external world and turn our attention inwards. That is where we will find the reality of every experience we live.

The next yama, not stealing, is common to many cultures on earth. Beyond the obvious meaning of taking what is not ours, stealing can be understood as separating ourselves from others. In this sense it is related to non violence. Our entire world is divided and we all compete with our neighbors whether it is a country, another city or the guy next door. When we are in a yoga class we try to do the pose better than the person next to us. Competition is separation and an act of stealing. Only one can be number one, while the others have to do without.

Just like the previous yamas, competition will be seen as something needed as long as we believe we are a body. As a body we live our lives outwards, by comparing our bodies to other bodies, and our body situation to other body situations. When the focus is turned inwards, the experience changes. Internally we crave for union not separation, for sharing not stealing. This does not mean we should give things away. If we let others take things from us, we are implicitly saying that what we have is not important and that is not true either. We must share as conscious and willing participants, not coerced. We will share with some people and protect ourselves from others. As non violence teaches us this is neither good nor bad. This is just how things are.

Don't lust is also common to multiple cultures or religions in the world. More orthodox translations of this sutra point to a life of abstinence, although the nature of the yamas point towards a different view. The yamas are insatiable. That is the main characteristic they share and why they must be avoided. If we get caught in the vicious cycle of sex, envy, lying, stealing, or harming, our desire will have no end. No matter how much we have, we will always want more.

The focus should not be so much on the activity itself but in not wanting it. It is the insatiable desire associated with the yamas that must be avoided. Once more, a core concept in yoga comes to our rescue. For the yoga philosophy our physical body is our vehicle for enlightenment. If we practice abstinence we will be able to control the desire. If we are able to control our bodies, we will be able to fight the desire in our minds. The body is the conduit to our minds and as we learn to control it, we also gain control of our minds.

When translating aparigraha, or coveting, this term is usually related to material things. It is usually not seen as desire or the source of all suffering as in Buddhism. The key is to turn the attention inwards so other treasures become available to us which will help us not covet material things. We will see this idea in a following sutra.

When working on the yamas, we should not get obsessed about them. If we think about non violence in reference to our relationship to others, anything we do will help someone and hurt someone else. If we buy something at shop A, we are hurting shop B. Or we could argue that not shopping at shop B gives them information they can use to improve. In short, we could go nuts if we think too much about it. The yamas will help us to stop being selfish, to develop a clean intention and to become aware of others, and we should take advantage of them that way. They will help us to bring the focus inwards and see our lives from a different perspective.

The yamas can only be truly met once we are enlightened. Only then can we ensure that what we do is truly the best for everyone and therefore not hurting anybody. If an action is not hurting anybody on a universal scale, we are acting in synch with the universe. Our actions would be following the flow of life and would be in harmony with its transcendental purpose. When applied in this context the yamas become a great vow.

(2.32) shaucha santosha tapah svadhyaya ishvarapranidhana niyamah

(2.32) The five niyamas are: be clean, be thankful, be committed, be introspective and be trusting of a higher purpose.

Virtue without a transcendental context is unachievable. But we already knew that. The hero always sacrificed himself for the greater good. If there is no greater good, the heroic act becomes a selfish deed. The act did not change, just its transcendental context. The niyamas are followed for a transcendental purpose: to know ourselves or to achieve oneness. Following the niyamas to obtain recognition defeats the purpose.

The niyamas are more complex than the yamas. First we had to avoid something that we were drawn towards. Now we have to consciously act. This step requires intention, not just restraint.

Being clean refers to the physical, mental and emotional aspects of ourselves. We all intuitively understand this concept and associate clean with simple and pure. Physically it refers to keeping the body clean outside as well as watching what we put into it. Mentally it refers to keeping the mind calm and watching our thoughts. Emotionally it refers to keeping our emotions under control and watching which emotional behaviors we allow ourselves. All levels are the same, each on their own context. All have external and internal aspects, and all levels require that we watch what we allow in.

Being thankful lets us see the positive in all things. Our thankfulness allows us to see the good side of a situation and take advantage of the lesson it contains. It is easy to be thankful for the good things in life, but thankfulness allows us also to see something painful with different eyes. When we give thanks for something hurtful we can look at it. Our pain was making us look away, shutting the experience down. Thankfulness is the way for us to open the lid and start to see what the experience was about. Only by looking at it will we be able to make sense of it, put it in perspective, and understand how that painful experience also made us who we are today. Thankfulness will help us to integrate the painful aspects of our lives and take the positive side of them, which exists in everything.

We take for granted that anything that happens in our lives contains a lesson we can learn. We live in a universe full of information and opportunity and being thankful is the way to tap into that well. Every time we feel hurt we cut that flow, denying us the experience and information that comes along with it. Being thankful is our way of reclaiming the life we have lived which we have not yet fully integrated into ourselves. If we go through a traumatic experience and we shut it down, we are denying ourselves the opportunity to grow from it. Being thankful is our way to reconnect to that event and allow it to help us be more.

As they say "If you stand for nothing you will fall for anything". Being committed means to take a stance, to make up our minds and to fight for something. It is easy to be committed for something tangible, like a country or a cause. It is harder to be committed to achieve enlightenment. Commitment must be combined with non judgment when pursuing enlightenment. Our quest must be the relentless pursuit of reality. This is the goal that we must aspire to and anything, even our preferences, beliefs or ideas are secondary to it. Commitment must be applied to continuously challenging ourselves, and questioning at all times whether what we think is correct or not. A life of commitment to enlightenment is a life of continuous search, adjustment, and looking where others do not dare look.

Introspection points to another key point in the sutras. Everything we are looking for we already have inside ourselves. We must see the outside world as the result, reaction, interaction or projection of what we are inside. Everything that happens to us is a result of us. The event was due to us, the understanding of the event was due to us, the ability to integrate it was due to us and our memory of it is due to us.

Introspection requires us to see the universe composed by two beings, one being us, and the other being everything else. Introspection is the interaction we have with everything else as a whole. As we live our lives inwardly, we are placing everything else outside. But all that is outside is what we need to interact with. If we only live inwardly, we only know what is in our heads. We cannot tell if what we think is real. Reality comes from interacting with the universe.

We must realize that our experience is internal, but we must pursue our interaction with what is outside us. This interaction is going to break the layers we have built between ourselves and the world and will allow us to question what we deem to be true. Questioning our beliefs is key in our path as an evolving being.

Finally, the last niyama, "ishvara-pranidhana", or trusting a higher purpose appears in multiple sutras. It was introduced in sutra 1.23, mentioned in 1.37 and 1.51, and opens Book 2 as one of the practices of kriya yoga, or yoga in action. Surrendering to a higher power in its passive understanding is related to non judgment and the acceptance of all facets of life. In its active understanding it relates to purposefully following the right path. In both definitions, surrendering is related to both yamas and niyamas.

We already do this. Maybe we don't identify it with a higher purpose but we already have this experience in our lives. We get to experience this through love. Every time we make an effort for a loved one we are surrendering our preferences for the benefit of someone else. Since we don't think that they are a higher power we don't realize that this is ishvara-pranidhana but it actually is. When we look at life from the perspective of introspection and see the entire universe as a single being, we can understand how an effort for a loved one can be considered ishvara-pranidhana. The fact that the effort was required by a particular person is not as important as the internal experience of overruling our preferences for something outside of us.

(2.33) vitarka badhane pratipaksha bhavanam (2.34) vitarkah himsadayah krita karita anumoditah lobha krodha moha purvakah mridu madhya adhimatrah dukha ajnana ananta phala iti pratipaksha bhavanam

(2.33) Don't let the wrong mindset prevent you from practicing the yamas and niyamas. If that is the case, turn your mindset around to help you achieve them. (2.34) The wrong mindset may make you hurt others; arises from greed, hate or stupidity; can be mild, moderate or acute, but it always brings sorrow. This is why one must always cultivate the right mindset.

Cultivating the right mindset could have been a limb all by itself. It is the cornerstone for both yamas and niyamas. This right mindset can take many forms, but the end result is what counts. The motivations that cause us to follow these practices are not important. Nor does it matter if we deem them good or bad, enlightened or low, clever or stupid. The important thing is that we follow the practices. As we evolve, our mindsets will evolve as will our motivations.

Nowadays we blame the ego for not having the right mindset. The reasons may be greed, hate or stupidity, but we still blame the ego. It is actually very convenient to have egos in these situations so we can put the blame elsewhere. As sutra 1.1 said, now is the time. We have given ourselves enough excuses not to do so many things. We need to find excuses to do them.

Following yamas and niyamas will feel as a burden and an effort at first. That is simply because we have other habits. We accept changing our habits in our professional lives but we have a harder time in our personal ones. We gladly accept management training, learning the habits of effective people or looking for cheese someone moved. The sutras provide a methodology towards samadhi but we don't feel like following them as much as professional learning because maybe we don't see the reward. A better job means more money and we associate that with a better life. We understand this concept of a better life so we understand the reward waiting for us.

When we start working on ourselves we don't really know what the reward is going to be. The first steps we take in this path are usually the result of dissatisfaction. What we have does not work anymore so we start looking for something else. It is only after a while that we want to continue for other reasons. The main thread throughout this path is the desire to keep searching. This desire is the basis of the mindset we want to cultivate. As we change, the mindset will take many forms but the motivation will always be the desire to know.

(2.35) ahimsa pratishthayam tat vaira-tyagah

(2.35) When you are deeply rooted in non harming others, your mere presence brings peace.

We have seen this kind of thing happen. Someone walks into a room and suddenly the vibe gets all weird. Or, if we have been in a stressful situation and the person who can help walks into the room, the vibe relaxes because we know she can take care of it.

We all carry a vibe, something like a radio signal that emanates from us and has a certain frequency. We can have a peaceful frequency or a stressed out frequency. The goal is to become an extreme case of not harming anyone and respecting everything so when we walk into a room everyone can feel the peace we carry with us.

(2.36) satya pratisthayam kriya phala ashrayatvam

(2.36) When making decisions based on reality, your course of action is guaranteed to be the most appropriate.

That is why knowledge is power. It is actionable and the outcome will be advantageous. This applies at all levels, from a sports game to a critical life decision. The goal of knowledge is not theoretical. Its purpose is to be put into action.

At the same time, by testing the knowledge on a practical level we confirm that we are correct. Only if a spiritual truth can be applied to our lives in a practical manner can we know that it is in fact correct and we understand it properly. Physical reality is the purpose and the test bed of all spiritual knowledge.

(2.37) asteya pratisthayam sarva ratna upasthanam

(2.37) When you stop wanting material things, more valuable jewels become available to you.

This is what happens when priorities change. As we search for more meaning in our lives the focus switches from outside to inside. We start valuing things like knowledge, experience, feeling good with ourselves, being able to enjoy life or having meaningful relationships. None of these are material. The fruition of all these depends on our ability to put knowledge into action. Happiness is a gauge that indicates how well we have understood and applied this knowledge.

In our culture we are told that if we have the house, the car and the job, we will be happy. Probably by now most of us have realized that this formula does not work. The solution has been there for a long time but was not in the mainstream. Confucius said: "Choose a job you love and you will never have to work a day in your life." Joe Campbell said: "Follow your bliss." And Sir Ken Robinson called it The Element in his book about finding that which inspires us and makes us happy. Happiness does not come from a static situation but from an active and creative process.

Following our bliss and happiness go hand in hand. Happiness is the way to find what we should be doing and if happiness is lost, that is the signal to find something else to do. Our bliss not only brings happiness but puts our entire lives in perspective. Once we are following our bliss, we will not just be looking for a mate, we will be looking for the mate with whom to follow our bliss. Same applies to our professional occupation, where we live, our hobbies and our friends.

Our bliss, what we should be doing in our lives, does not need to be enlightenment. There is a lot to do, all of which is meaningful. We do not need to devote our entire life to yoga or philosophy, but to take advantage of these to improve our lives. We should use what helps us in pursuing our bliss and discard the rest. Pursuing our bliss is even more important than pursuing samadhi. If we were able to come to this world incarnation after incarnation and pursue our bliss in each one of those lives, what would we want samadhi for? One day, after many lives, our bliss will be to pursue samadhi. Then we should work on it, but not sooner.

(2.38) brahmacharya pratisthayam virya labhah

(2.38) When you flow with the rhythm of life your life becomes effortless.

The concept of surrendering comes up again, this time as flowing with the rhythm of life. Surrendering can be seen in two ways, one passive and one active. The passive one has to do with accepting what is happening to us as though dictated by a higher power. In the west we call this divine providence or god's will. The passive view of surrendering also involves accepting everything as it is, regardless of whether we like it, understand it, or agree with it.

The active aspect requires a conscious action though, not just acceptance. The active aspect entails using our energies to follow the right path, do what we have to do. In a more refined view it means to flow with life, looking at our personal life from the perspective of the universal consciousness and acting accordingly.

A consequence of properly surrendering is having no regrets. If we are flowing with life and living the moment, there is no need to look back. What happened was meant to happen the way it did so there is no need to have second thoughts.

Surrendering lastly implies that we are totally accepted by the universal consciousness. We have free will and we can do whatever we want with it. Surrendering is a choice and not surrendering is also a choice, both of which are available to us. Whatever we do is ok. We will still have to deal with our lives and the consequences of how we live but we are definitely not offending any greater power in the process.

(2.39) aparigraha sthairye janma kathanta sambodhah

(2.39) When you follow a simple life, you will be able to find your true purpose.

As introduced in sutra 2.37, our purpose is our bliss. However, sometimes it is not that easy to find. For some of us finding our bliss is a bit of a riddle. We see that we have skills that we may not enjoy so much, and that which we like we cannot afford doing as a living. We need to work through the process of unveiling both our bliss and the process of making it feasible in our lives. This requires quiet time to realize what it is we have to do, quiet time to plan it and the energy to make it happen. If our lives are full of activities we will have neither the time nor the energy to devote to our life purpose.

(2.40) sauchat sva-anga jugupsa paraih asamsargah (2.41) sattva shuddhi saumanasya ekagra indriya-jaya atma darshana yogyatvani cha

(2.40) When you cleanse your body of toxins, emotional and physical, you will want to preserve this state of cleanliness (2.41) and with this cleanliness comes the ability to focus the mind, see the truth, control the senses and gain self realization.

Yoga is about removing. As we make our body cleaner by following these practices our lives will change. Jobs may change, friends may change or any other area in our lives may change until our outward life gets in synch with our internal one. Our life will improve and once the transition is complete we will cherish our new situation so much that we will not want to lose it. The way to do this is not by getting attached to the outward manifestation but to keep working on ourselves.

When we see the Zen monasteries we see simple and plain rooms, free of clutter. This is not by chance. The mind there can be calm and clean just as the room. Inside and outside are always in synch and this relationship goes both ways.

(2.42) santosha anuttamah sukha labhah

(2.42) When you are thankful for the things in your life, you will be happy.

Thankfulness is the way to feel happy as it allows us to see the glass half full. Thankfulness helps us see the positive, the useful side of what we have in front of us and it is a habit we can acquire. However there are deeper feelings and beliefs that cannot be corrected by thankfulness alone.

Being happy is a deeper feeling than feeling happy. Feeling happy we can obtain via thankfulness, but being happy is different. Being happy is the sign that we have connected with who we are and with what we are supposed to do on this Earth. Being happy is that deeper connection to our purpose. While feeling happy has a sense of excitement, being happy is more connected with satisfaction.

Happiness is our natural state. Look at children. How easy it is to make them laugh and smile, even in difficult situations. Unhappiness is the sign there is something inside we must get rid of as mentioned in sutra 1.31. Like a thorn in our side, a fear stuck inside will prevent us from being happy. We need to remove the false belief that created that fear or it will keep bugging us. Unhappiness is just a signal there is something in our heads we need to deal with.

(2.43) kaya indriya siddhih ashuddhi kshayat tapasah

(2.43) When you are dedicated and determined, you become master of your own body, taking control over it instead of being controlled by it.

We look at all the people in the gym building up their bodies and we judge them as misguided. However, we reward people who follow strenuous diets and see them as examples. Both are just different approaches at taking control of our bodies. They are neither good nor bad, they are only different ways. Whether they fall off the wagon or go over the top is entirely their own affair. The sutras recommend we cleanse our bodies and minds and offer us insight and practices to do so. How we do this is up to us. How someone else does it is up to them.

(2.44) svadhyayat ishta samprayogah (2.45) samadhi siddhih ishvarapranidhana

(2.44) When you study yourself, you can understand how the universe works. (2.45) When you know yourself, you become one with the universe.

As above so below. What this sutra says is that we are modeled according to the structure of the universe. Everything is ruled by the same laws and that's why studying ourselves is relevant to the universe. If we truly understood how we functioned at all levels we would understand how everything worked. If we understood one thing fully we could understand everything fully. Every single thing represents the whole. The fact that there are things we don't understand at all indicates that we don't fully understand anything.

(2.46) sthira sukham asanam (2.47) prayatna shaithilya ananta samapattibhyam

(2.46) Yoga postures (asanas) should be practiced by holding them for some time until they feel comfortable. (2.47) They should be practiced without expectation but focused so the mind is empty.

The word asana can refer both to all the yoga positions or just the posture used to meditate. What we usually call practicing yoga can be described as following a sequence of body poses and getting our body from one to the next. What this sutra recommends is that we hold the posture for some time. Anybody that has practiced yoga can attest to this. Unless we can hold the posture for a while we cannot really say that we can do the pose at all.

The benefits of the pose are realized only after being in it, not immediately, and unless we practice the posture many times we will not be able to feel comfortable. When we feel comfortable in the pose we know that we have extracted its benefits and it is time to try a harder one. So the sutra is also saying that we should work on asanas that are uncomfortable, and keep practicing them until they become easier. Only challenging asanas will provide a reward, so once we feel comfortable, we should move on and find a more challenging one to work on. The focus of the sutra is in the process, not in the end result. The benefit comes from walking the path, not in arriving at the destination.

Yoga pursues a real experience. While we stay in our thoughts that is all we will know, yet we will still be unable to tell if they are real or not. However, the body, its laws and processes are real. Putting the body through the practice will stir sensations, emotions and memories which are real. Asanas allow us to observe the body and from watching it gain wisdom. Sutra 1.38 suggests that we pay attention to our dreams. The reason is the same as for practicing asanas. Dreams are outside out mental processes and therefore have the potential to be real.

Regarding the meditation position, we need to hold it for a while as well. A steady and comfortable posture will provide the mind with a stable environment to meditate. The more asanas we practice and the more we challenge ourselves during our asana practice, the easier it will be to become comfortable while meditating.

The Zen expression "mushin no shin" – or mind without mind – refers to cultivating an empty mind. This is the state of mind that the samurai aimed at during combat and what we nowadays call being in the zone. Athletes work to obtain this focus during their performance, and an athlete with a strong mind is one who can get to this empty state at will. This is the state of mind we are aiming for during our asana practice as well.

(2.48) tatah dvandva anabhighata

(2.48) Through practice comes freedom from duality.

My wife has been practicing yoga for many years but for at least the last eight she has practiced every day for not less than two hours. That not only includes practicing during our vacations but also making special arrangements so she can practice the day we take the plane out or back. Two hours a day for eight years comes up to 5,840hrs. It would take someone practicing three hours a week a total of 37 years to practice the same amount. So when I asked her what she thought the sutras meant by being freed from duality this is what she said:

> "When you practice for a long time you realize that body and mind are not separate. You need the mind to do the posture. Where you are focusing your attention in your body will make you get the posture or not. If you are thinking about something else you will not do as well. But it also goes the other way. When working in a posture, fear comes up at certain points. This fear sometimes comes after years of practicing the same move. It is as if by practicing you have released the fear from its cage. Then, as you get to work through the fear, it goes away. The fear seems unrelated to the asana, but a very specific fear always comes up with the same pose. Then, when you work on it during your practice, you clear it out from your everyday life as well"

Something else I have learned from watching her practice is that she is not deterred by pain. Pain is just the sign that she needs to work either more, or in a more clever way. There are different kinds of pain, she says, so taking care of her body is essential but unless it feels like an injury, she keeps going. Her commitment (2.32) to explore the limits of the body and mind has blurred the lines between pain and pleasure and these are not seen as good and bad anymore. Work is seen as good, and laziness (sutra 1.30) as bad, that is for certain. She always says that her practice is her best teacher and it is easy to see how practicing the way she does naturally aligns with so many principles in the sutras.

(2.49) tasmin sati shvasa prashvsayoh gati vichchhedah pranayamah

(2.49) Observing and controlling the inhaling and exhaling of the breath during the asana is called pranayama.

There are two main physiological cycles in the body: blood and air. In the blood cycle, the heart moves blood around the body, oxygenating it in the lungs and sending it back out to the cells. In the air cycle, the lungs inhale in, use oxygen to clean the blood and then carbon dioxide is exhaled out. For the west, the blood cycle is most important and the breath is seen as supporting the heart. For the east, the air cycle is the most important and the heart is doing its customary job.

For the eastern tradition, breathing can help us control the energy in the body. Pranayama is made of two Sanskrit words, prana and ayam. Prana is the universal energy and ayam means to extend, draw out, or release. Through breathing we can release the prana, making it circulate throughout our bodies. Prana is everywhere in the environment, all around us and drives all the functions of the body. It corresponds to chi or ki in Chinese or Japanese traditions. In the yoga tradition the prana travels through nadis. Nadis are to prana what veins are to blood, but prana being energy, the nadis are energetic channels.

Meditations and visualizations have become more popular lately with the so called new age movement. Hearing someone tell us to inhale white light into our heart centers is not so strange anymore. Then afterwards, the visualization usually does something with that light. We either expand it, or send it to an area in our body that needs help. This is what we would do with prana. This white light is our western version of prana or chi or ki. We don't usually identify it as universal energy, we call it instead pure white light or something similar.

(2.50) bahya abhyantara stambha vrittih desha kala sankhyabhih paridrishtah dirgha sukshmah

(2.50) You can make your breath longer and more subtle by varying the three aspects of breathing: inhalation, exhalation or retention. You can vary the length, how many times you do each, or the area of the body you are focusing on.

In the yoga tradition there are currents of prana in the body. Like currents in the ocean. These currents describe the overall movement of prana inside our physical body. These currents are called vayus. The two most important are the prana and the apana vayus. The prana vayu consists of an expansion of prana in the body, which happens during inhale. The act of inhaling is an outward movement as our chest fills with air. The apana vayu is the opposite and has a contracting action. Apana is associated with elimination and grounding.

During the prana vayu the body expands like the flowers and leaves in a tree both bloom and gather light. This expansion of prana is a collection of new information, new energy and new possibilities. During the inhale air comes in, while the body stretches out.

The apana vayu releases the air, keeps what can be used and discards the rest. It digests and integrates new information and roots us more into reality. This is the tree in autumn after losing all the leaves, getting ready for winter. This cycle concentrates and compensates the prana vayu.

During this cycle we are drawn inwards to assimilate what should be kept and eliminate what is not needed.

While air is coming in and out, prana is moving around and we feel okay. It is during the retention where the problem is. If we try holding the air out for a long time, the mind panics. It feels as if we are going to die although we know we have control over inhaling again. When we stop the flow is when we create the problem. The same happens in our lives, trouble comes when we get stuck.

(2.51) bahya abhyantara vishaya akshepi chaturthah (2.52) tatah kshiyate prakasha avaranam

(2.51) There is a fourth aspect to breathing, a more subtle one, in which you gather prana not through the nostrils but at an energetic level. (2.52) Through this last aspect of pranayama, your false beliefs can dissolve and disappear.

When we inhale we activate the prana vayu, the expanding of prana in the body, but we cannot assure that prana is coming in just through the nose. After all, prana being energy, it should have more freedom to move around. This sutra talks about a fourth aspect of pranayama in which we take prana directly in, via a conscious intake. Since prana is energy, it is our intention that draws it in.

This fourth approach is also similar to the western visualization where we take white light into the body and then project it out. The intake of the energy is not necessarily through the nose but at an energetic level. When sufficiently relaxed we may feel the tingling in the body which signals that something is moving. We cannot see air with the eyes but we know that there is something happening because the lungs fill up. In the same way, we can tell prana is moving when we feel the tingling in the body.

(2.53) dharanasu cha yogyata manasah

(2.53) Through these pranayama practices, the mind gets trained to focus and concentrate.

As mentioned in sutra 1.36, mind and breath are two fish swimming together. When we control one we control the other. These fish follow each other exactly. If we want to focus the mind, focus the breath. To relax the mind, relax the breath. To make the mind go deeper, deepen the breath. To put the mind in suspension, hold the breath. To appreciate life, take a full breath in and breathe out with satisfaction.

This goes the other way as well. When we are anxious our breath is short and shallow and when calm our breath is relaxed. That is why sutra 1.31 says that we are suffering the consequences of the nine obstacles if we have difficulty breathing in a steady manner.

(2.54) sva vishaya asamprayoge chittasya svarupe anukarah iva indriyanam pratyaharah(2.55) tatah parama vashyata indriyanam

(2.54) When you focus and concentrate internally so much that you forget you have a body, as if the senses were on pause, that is called pratyahara. (2.55) Then you can have control over how you relate to the world.

A state where we lose awareness of the body is described in Robert Monroe's books on astral traveling. Monroe recommends using deep relaxation of both body and mind to get to this state. He describes this state as a void in which our only source of stimulation is our own thoughts since all awareness of the body is gone.

In yoga philosophy the senses are more than the five senses that we know in the west. What we translate as senses they call indriyas, and they are ways to interact with the world. Five indriyas take the world in, and the other five are actions on the world. Our five senses – seeing, smelling, tasting, hearing and feeling – are the five cognitive indriyas. With them we gather information about the world. The other five help us express ourselves and are the active indriyas. These are eliminating, reproducing, moving, grabbing and speaking.

It is controlling all these ten that the sutra talks about. As Frank Herbert said in his famous novel Dune: "He who can destroy a thing, controls a thing." The approach is comparable in this sutra. When we can put the activity of the indriyas on hold, we can control them.

End of the Commentaries to Book 2

Book 3: The Internal Practices (Vibhuti Pada)

Interpretation of Book 3

(3.1) Concentration is the ability to focus the mind on an object for a period of time. (3.2) When concentration makes the entire mind absorbed in the object so everything else disappears, that is meditation. (3.3) When you feel connected to the object, as if you both were one, it is an experience comparable to samadhi (oneness). (3.4) When these three are combined, we call it absorbed connection – or samyama. (3.5) By using absorbed connection, you can learn the true nature of things (3.6) but practice in stages, building up one step at a time. (3.7) These last three practices are more internal than the previous five (3.8) but even these last three are external in relation to pure samadhi (oneness).

(3.9) Build the ability of consciously dropping bad habits and stopping the acquisition of false beliefs. (3.10) Once used to it, this exercise becomes effortless. (3.11) Build the ability to keep the mind focused, not scattered; (3.12) as well as the ability to equally look at both the positive and negative aspects in all things. (3.13) These three abilities determine how you see the world.

(3.14) Before something is in the "now", it is in a state of "about to happen." The moment right after "now" contains the future, in an "about to happen" state. (3.15) Reality is a sequence of independent events that consciousness sees as continuous. (3.16) An absorbed connection (samyama) with this nature of time gives you knowledge of the past and the future.

(3.17) An absorbed connection with the distinction of an object, the idea representing it, and the word naming it gives you knowledge of all languages. (3.18) With your current belief system gives you knowledge of your past lives, (3.19) and with other people's minds lets you understand them, (3.20) but does not give the reasons why they think what they think, or why they are the way they are.

(3.21) An absorbed connection with the form of your own body makes the eye unable to capture the reflected light and you become invisible. (3.22) The same can be done regarding the body being heard, touched, tasted or smelled.

(3.23) Karma is fast or slow to manifest; an absorbed connection with your actions or received omens brings knowledge about your own death.

(3.24) An absorbed connection with friendliness and similar qualities develops them in yourself; (3.25) with the strength of an elephant lets you know it's strength; (3.26) and with a remote object lets you learn its whereabouts and situation.

(3.27) An absorbed connection with the sun gives you knowledge about the structure of the universe; (3.28) with the moon lets you learn about the stars; (3.29) and with the pole star lets you learn about the movement of the stars.

(3.30) An absorbed connection with the navel chakra teaches you the physiology of the body (3.31) and with the throat chakra lets you get rid of hunger and thirst. (3.32) An absorbed connection with the turtle channel gives you poise.

(3.33) An absorbed connection with the light on the top of the head lets you learn about the masters.

(3.34) Or all of these can come at once, in a flash of intuition.

(3.35) An absorbed connection with the heart teaches you about the nature of your own mind.

(3.36) The expression of an object and the consciousness that enables it to exist are so intimately intertwined that we believe the object can exist without the consciousness behind it. An absorbed connection with the consciousness that allows reality to express itself through our senses teaches you about that consciousness. (3.37) And from the understanding of this consciousness you can develop higher or transcendental senses. (3.38) However, all these extraordinary abilities – siddhis – are actually obstacles to attaining samadhi.

(3.39) As you understand the reasons for physical reality to exist and understand how consciousness comes into the body, the association between mind and body becomes less fixed. They are then able to decouple and you can enter other bodies. (3.40) When you understand the upward flow of prana in your body, you can achieve levitation. (3.41) When you master the flow of prana in the navel area, you become full of life and power.

(3.42) An absorbed connection with the relationship between hearing and the ether gives you extrasensory hearing, (3.43) and with the relationship between the body and ether, as well as on the lightness of cotton, lets you teleport your body.

(3.44) When you realize that everything you see is you, not something outside yourself, you can de-identify from your body. An absorbed connection with this concept lets you understand your spiritual being.

(3.45) An absorbed connection with the realization that objects are the result of the interaction of the primordial elements lets you master these elements. (3.46) Through the mastery of the elements, you can make your body perfect, small at will, indestructible, and bring about other exceptional characteristics.(3.47) This perfection includes beauty, grace, strength and the resistance of a diamond.

(3.48) An absorbed connection with the senses (indriyas), their processes, nature, relationship to each other and their purpose lets you understand them and how they function. (3.49) With the mastery over the senses you can perceive and interact with the world without using the physical instruments in the body.

(3.50) Through the understanding of the difference between the object and the consciousness that makes that object possible, comes omniscience and omnipotence.

(3.51) If you can free yourself from these achievements, you can attain absolute freedom. (3.52) Don't be proud of your achievements even when being recognized by those you look up to since you may take a step back in your spiritual path.

(3.53) Finally, an absorbed connection with the succession of infinitesimal continuous moments, which is time, gives you intuitive knowledge (3.54) and with this knowledge you understand how everything is unique and unrepeatable. (3.55) Also, you become able to transcend time and space and understand the whole of creation, everywhere and everywhen. (3.56) Once you realize the holiness of everything you see, you can attain total liberation.

End of Interpretation of Book 3

Commentary to Book 3

(3.1) deshah bandhah chittasya dharana (3.2) tatra pratyaya ekatanata dhyanam (3.3) tad eva artha matra nirbhasam svarupa shunyam iva samadhih

(3.1) Concentration is the ability to focus the mind on an object for a period of time. (3.2) When concentration makes the entire mind absorbed in the object so everything else disappears, that is meditation. (3.3) When you feel connected to the object, as if you both were one, it is an experience comparable to samadhi (oneness).

Chapter 3 starts introducing the last three limbs of yoga: concentration, meditation and samadhi. Concentration and meditation are more of the mind while the last one, samadhi, is emotional. Connecting to something is an emotional process.

The limbs started with behaviors (yamas and niyamas), then moved to physical practices (asana, pranayama and pratyahara) and end with the mind and emotions. This order is not arbitrary but follows an progression. To follow a behavior we don't really need to understand it, just the will to follow it. When it comes to physical practices we need to make a larger effort since now we are feeling the effects of the practice in our own bodies. Finally we need to control our minds and emotions. With each limb there is a higher level of maturity required as each limb is more personal and subtle.

The yoga tradition has organized our human activities as well as given them a methodology and a purpose. If we are having trouble concentrating let's say, we need to evaluate where we are with all the limbs before concentration. Once we get them in order we will be in a better position to fix our concentration problem. If we try to tackle our concentration issue without addressing our behaviors (yamas or niyamas) or control over our bodies (asanas) we will make little progress.

(3.4) trayam ekatra samyama (3.5) tad jayat prajna lokah (3.6) tasya bhumisu viniyogah

(3.4) When these three are combined, we call it absorbed connection – or samyama. (3.5) By using absorbed connection, you

can learn the true nature of things (3.6) but practice in stages, building up one step at a time.

Samyama, or absorbed connection, is the main theme of this chapter. It combines mind and emotion to connect with a single object. This emotional bond allows for information to flow in regarding the object we connect with. The nature of the bonded object is open to us and we can receive as much as we allow. An emotional connection is a trusting exercise. We need to open to the object we are working with if we want to make the connection.

The key of samyama is to connect and identify with the object or concept we are working with. Something similar to samyama is used in the west when working with goals. Some goal coaches tell us to imagine ourselves as if we had already achieved our goal, to imagine us being successful. Then they ask to literally go into our successful self and feel the vibe, the energy imprint of that successful version of ourselves. This is how absorbed connection or samyama works. We need to become one with the object we are working with. Get the vibe, connect. Goal setting is just a specific instance in which we connect to our future selves.

A list of samyama practices start with sutra 3.14 and make up the remainder of this third book. There are two sections of practices divided by a flash of intuition in sutra 3.34. From sutra 3.14 to sutra 3.33, the practices follow the evolutionary path, walking us through different stages. The flash represents an enlightenment moment. Then, from sutra 3.35 to the end – sutra 3.56 – the samyama practices describe how to achieve samadhi by undoing ourselves. The last samyama practice connects back to the first one, both involving the nature of time, reminding us of the cycle of life.

(3.7) trayam antar angam purvebhyah (3.8) tad api bahir angam nirbijasya

(3.7) These last three practices are more internal than the previous five (3.8) but even these last three are external in relation to pure samadhi (oneness).

These practices are in our heads or our hearts, therefore are internal. Concentration, meditation and connection to a single object are internal activities for which we can produce no physical proof. We can see the effects of these in our lives but we can only infer that we are concentrated by the expression in our faces.

However, these are still activities of our outer selves. Who we are is deeper than the part of us that concentrates, meditates or connect to one thing. Pure samadhi, the connection to all, is achieved at a deeper level than our mental or emotional bodies.

(3.9) vyutthana nirodhah samskara abhibhava pradurbhavau nirodhah ksana chitta anvayah nirodhah-parinamah (3.10) tasya prashanta vahita samskarat (3.11) sarvarathata ekagrata ksaya udaya chittasya samadhi-parinamah (3.12) tatah punah shanta-uditau tulya-pratyayau chittasya ekagrata-parinamah (3.13) etena bhuta indriyasau dharma laksana avastha parinamah vyakhyatah

(3.9) Build the ability of consciously dropping bad habits and stopping the acquisition of false beliefs. (3.10) Once used to it, this exercise becomes effortless. (3.11) Build the ability to keep the mind focused, not scattered; (3.12) as well as the ability to equally look at both the positive and negative aspects in all things. (3.13) These three abilities determine how you see the world.

These three skills are the single most useful idea in the whole sutras. The sutras call these skills "abilities", as in something we need to develop. The first one consists in consciously dropping or acquiring beliefs on purpose, called nirodhah-parinamah. This is a powerful skill to have. Imagine if we can drop the belief that we need something that is bothering us. Or if we can drop the need to have something we don't have. This skill can cure our need to have food, alcohol, sex or money. It can also correct our need to feel this or that way. How much more control over our lives we would have if we had this skill.

As we work on our belief system we get cleaner inside which helps us judge new things by how they resonate within us. Correct beliefs intuitively feel right and once we experience one we want more of them. Our ability to detect falseness increases and our tolerance for fallacy decreases. As we get cleaner it does become effortless in that it becomes unavoidable. We have a harder time being around certain people and we gravitate towards others.

The second skill, samadhi-parinamah , recommends us to develop a focused mind. Working on our minds is the easiest of the three in our current society. Mind is king, so any field of study will help us with this task. The key of this skill is to totally focus on what we are doing while we are on it. At work only think about work. At home only think about home. When talking to a friend only think about our friend. This skill is essential to conserve our energies.

Finally, for the third ability, ekagrata-parinamah, we need to see both the positive and negative sides of things. Nowadays, our efforts will have to be towards finding the positive. The media already focuses enough on the negative thus making our minds follow, so effort will have to be made towards seeing the positive side of things. Once we can see both the good and the bad in all, everything becomes purposeful. Everything has a reason to be where it is and provides us with information. This last ability will make us analyze our environment and our lives, giving us a deeper relationship to everything we interact with.

(3.14) shanta udita avyapadeshya dharma anupati dharmi (3.15) krama anyatvam parinamah anyatve hetu (3.16) parinimah traya samyama atita anagata jnana

(3.14) Before something is in the "now", it is in a state of "about to happen." The moment right after "now" contains the future, in an "about to happen" state. (3.15) Reality is a sequence of independent events that consciousness sees as continuous. (3.16) An absorbed connection (samyama) with this nature of time gives you knowledge of the past and the future.

This is the first of the samyama or absorbed connection practices. Time represents physical reality, time is physical reality. The sutras remind us that we are immersed in time and that we need to deal with it. The ability to gain knowledge of the past and future represents the restlessness and uncertainty we feel in learning to deal with this place. This exercise is vague, almost representing the moment before coming to this physical universe for the first time.

I have not seen any translation explaining these sutras this way but this concept of time is not unique. Australian aborigines have probably the most sophisticated concept of time of all cultures on earth and they basically describe the same idea. Their concept of time affects our understanding of physical reality since our entire physical experience becomes a consequence of time.

This phenomenon has also been seen in quantum physics. The most elementary particles blink in and out of reality. The connection that physics has not yet made is that blinking is what makes time and physical reality move forward and exist. An object is not just a bunch of atoms held together in a structure. An object is a sequence of blinks of its elementary particles that create a different object in each of its blinks. Consciousness is aware of the blink we call "now" so we think the object static. However, the object is traveling through space blinking many times per second. It is as if reality was a humongous 3D movie in which we live. Each of the 3D frames contains a 3D picture of the entire universe, and the sequence of 3D frames is what we call reality and time.

The next blink is known to the universe. The next blink is so close to the "now" that the universe knows what version of the future to move our consciousness to so it can produce the next "now." "Now" is defined as the blink that our consciousness is aware of. The same idea exists in the Aboriginal concept of time. By practicing samyama on this concept of time we can learn about the past and the future. We would be connecting to the time web and be able to see the possible and actual pasts and futures.

These practical exercises set yoga apart from other philosophies. Yoga is practical in two senses. First, it recognizes our physical vehicle, our body, to be our vehicle for enlightenment. This makes yoga unique. Secondly, it presents a set of practices, like these samyama practices, that will allow us to evaluate our progress. We will know that we are truly understanding the theory only when we can put it into practice. This second point is comparable to the practices of the Tibetan monks who live in caves and devote their lives to their spiritual practices.

(3.17) shabda artha pratyaya itaretara adhyasat samkara tat pravibhaga samyama sarva bhuta ruta jnana

(3.17) An absorbed connection with the distinction of an object, the idea representing it, and the word naming it gives you knowledge of all languages.

One of the first things we learn to do is to speak. Our language gives us a sense of belonging and identity. It determines the place where we are about to start our life. This second absorbed connection exercise represents the coming to this world and learning to get acquainted with it.

Regarding the exercise, languages should be an attainable skill to acquire. Language is human made and as such resides in the human collective mind. A collective mind is a plausible explanation to the known hundredth monkey effect. This effect was discovered by scientists conducting experiments on monkeys on a Japanese island. They observed how one of the monkeys learned to wash its food. This behavior spread to the younger monkeys and once the population of monkeys that washed their food became large enough, others in close by islands began to do the same. The interesting thing is that these monkeys on the second island had no direct contact with the first ones. It is as if the knowledge gained by one is stored in a common repository from which all members of the group can benefit. Once a critical mass is reached, all the members of the group have access to that skill.

Like any other human skill, our languages would be stored in the shared human repository, the collective human mind. If we can tap into it we could pick up skills that others learned for the group. By practicing an absorbed connection with any skill we should be able to download it by connecting to the collective mind.

It is not clear from the text if we should think of a particular object, like a table, and its associated word and idea, or if we should think about objects, words and ideas as abstract entities. Notice also, that the exercise does not tell us to focus on the result we are looking for. The skill we can gain comes as a consequence of something else. In this case by practicing an absorbed connection with an object, word and idea we gain knowledge of languages. We do not practice samyama with the language, but obtain the language as a result of focusing on another topic. This approach is recurrent in all absorbed connection exercises.

(3.18) samskara saksat karanat purva jati jnanam

(3.18) [An absorbed connection] with your current belief system gives you knowledge of your past lives.

This exercise represents reincarnation, all the lives we live and the knowledge we gain through them. Our personal history holds the experiences that make us what we are. The sutras, being from the east, regard reincarnation as the way we evolve, coming back to the world over and over. This fact is a given throughout the sutras.

This samyama practice implies that there is always a reason for how we are, how we behave and our current belief system. We are not a blank slate when we are born, we bring a history with us. Our past experiences and our ability to integrate our past into ourselves will determine our current belief system.

If our current belief system is the result of our past lives, we should pay special attention to our beliefs during this life because they will affect our next. Our beliefs are a true treasure. They are something we can literally take to the grave with us. Our belief system measures our progress in understanding the universe and measures our spiritual development stage. We have the chance to evolve and improve our spirit by carefully improving our belief system.

We can see simple examples of this idea in regular people. Some people act as if they have enough and others as if they never do, sometimes to an extent that cannot be explained by their known past. Having or not having enough is a core belief that will affect most of what we do in life. This belief is intimately related to our understanding of the universe and how it works. A view of limited resources would give us a belief system of not having enough while a perspective of abundance would create the opposite.

(3.19) pratyayasya para chitta jnana (3.20) na cha tat salambana tasya avisayin bhutatvat

(3.19) and [an absorbed connection] with other people's minds lets you understand them, (3.20) but does not give the reasons why they think what they think, or why they are the way they are.

The next step in our evolution is to start understanding others, to realize that there are people around us with whom we need to coexist. We call this empathy, imagining how the world looks from someone else's shoes. Empathy allows us to understand someone else's point of view by figuratively becoming them. This is part of samyama, becoming one with the subject of the exercise.

This exercise will also help us to look at others with better eyes. As illogical as some people's decisions may seem from the outside, they were made from a place that made sense to them. It may have been fear, a painful past experience or a false belief what made them behave the way they did. Either way, there is always a logical explanation and this exercise will help us relate.

While we can know their mind we cannot know their history. Our karma and our history is our personal business. If someone practiced samyama on us, they could understand how we behave and how our minds work, but not why we are the way we are. Seems that there are still some things we are meant to learn with a good old fashioned conversation.

(3.21) kaya rupa samyama tat grahya shakti tat stambhe chaksuh prakasha asamprayoga antardhanam (3.22) etena shabdadi antardhanam uktam

(3.21) An absorbed connection with the form of your own body makes the eye unable to capture the reflected light and you become invisible. (3.22) The same can be done regarding the body being heard, touched, tasted or smelled.

Manipulating our environment is the next phase in our evolutionary path. This absorbed connection exercise is manipulating how others perceive us. Nowadays this could be achieved via technology or marketing. Both can actually change how we are perceived by others.

While the samyama exercises describe an evolutionary path, we should consider that they are actually achievable and maybe we can figure out how to become invisible. Now, think of those hypnotism shows where a hypnotist makes people unable to see something. We can find some easily online these days. There is this one where the hypnotized person just stops seeing the hypnotist. The question that always bugged me was: how did the hypnotized person see what was behind the hypnotist? According to physics, light bounces around, the eye catches it and we see things. If the body of the hypnotist is still there and it is just the one person who cannot see him, how could that person see through the hypnotist? According to this sutra, the eye is not able to capture the light that is bouncing off our body anymore and that is why we become invisible. However, the light reflected on the objects behind us while we are invisible is making it now to the eye of the one looking. Either light is already going through us and the brain organizes the final picture setting up things in front of each other, or we don't really see by capturing reflected light that comes straight at us. Unless we challenge some of the widely accepted laws of physics, the hypnotist trick cannot be explained.

The sutra goes then to list the other senses, so although they cannot see us, they can still touch us. If we could avoid being touched, we could potentially walk through walls. And that is the thing about these samyama exercises. They are impossible for us to believe. However, if we doubt their credibility, wouldn't we also be doubting the rest of the book along with the possibility of enlightenment? It is quite bold of the sutras to list a set of exercises that involve invisibility or walking through walls, but these are the siddhis. Siddhis are akin to superpowers we acquire once we are able to truly understand and put into practice the yoga teachings. Actually that is their sole use, to tell us that we are on the right path.

(3.23) sopakramam nirupakramam cha karma tat samyama aparanta jnanam aristebhyah va

(3.23) Karma is fast or slow to manifest; an absorbed connection with your actions or received omens brings knowledge about your own death.

While the previous absorbed connection exercise dealt with manipulating perception, this one deals with the occult, represented by death. We can see that today's world is mostly in the previous stage. We have cosmetic surgery to alter our bodies while marketing and drug companies alter our minds. The world has had a couple of attempts at moving to the next stage, a more mystical or esoteric take on the world, but that has not happened yet. The beginning of the 20th century was a very esoteric time with Blavatsky, Bailey, Bardon, Leadbeater, Krishnamurti or Gurdjieff. Then the wars came. However, with the abundance of population in the world today, we could probably say that there are more people today interested in mysticism than there were then, although the percentage to the total population may be smaller.

Having multiple possible futures is a logical deduction of the explanation of time in sutra 3.14. Based on the actions we take, our consciousness travels down one of the possible future paths making that path the "now" and making it history. Our current actions are putting us on a path that could be predicted and this absorbed connection exercise taps into the fabric of time and locks on the path that we will follow given our current actions.

Omens are like traffic signs that tell us what road we are traveling. They either tell us that we are traveling down the preferred road, the right path, or tell us to change paths. These omens that we see now were set up in the past. This means that there is a purpose or an ideal outcome for our lives. Unless there was a preferred end, omens could not be set up front. Some futures get omens to confirm the right path, and other futures get the wrong path's omens. When we reflect on our already received omens via samyama we can infer what path we are on and foresee our own death.

(3.24) maitri dishu balani

(3.24) An absorbed connection with friendliness and similar qualities develops them in yourself;

The stage after mysticism is true personal growth: friendliness. Being able to develop friendliness requires raising our personal frequency or vibe. We are truly changing ourselves and our energetic imprint.

This samyama exercise is comparable to the goal setting example mentioned before but it goes further. While success is achieved outwards, friendliness is accomplished internally. Practicing an absorbed connection with a quality as pure as friendliness will cause our vibration level to increase. This exercise is the first true self development exercise. Until now we have been dealing with the outside world and learning how to deal with it. Now we are finally targeting our true self.

(3.25) baleshu hasti baladini

(3.25) [An absorbed connection] with the strength of an elephant lets you know it's strength;

This samyama practice wants to remind us that as we progress in the path, things get harder not easier. The elephant represents the steady course that we need to follow in order to achieve our goal. We must not falter or give up. Once we start working on ourselves, our demons are going to come up and we will need the strength of an elephant to deal with them and keep going.

Ganesha, the elephant god is the patron of yoga. He reminds us to never give up. He also reminds us to keep a light attitude. He is a fat dude with the head of an elephant who travels on a mouse, which if we think about it is pretty funny. Ganesha has a big belly, representing his developed hara center. The hara is the center of gravity of the body and the seat of enlightenment.

(3.26) pravrittyah aloka nyasat suksma vyavahita viprakrista jnanam

(3.26) and [an absorbed connection] with a remote object lets you learn its whereabouts and situation.

The remote object represents our goal: enlightenment, liberation or samadhi. We must keep an eye on the target and keep advancing towards it. This absorbed connection exercise tells us to practice with a remote object, reminding us to focus on the long term goal. Enlightenment and oneness are not the same, but certainly are in the same direction from where we are standing.

On the physical level, we call this remote viewing. The Australian Aborigines are known for having a similar skill. All of them can go into a light trance state and get messages from people away from them, or know if someone is coming, or get information to go to a different place. This is not a witchery trick, it is a common skill they all know how to develop and everyone in the tribe knows how to do.

(3.27) bhuvana jnanam surya samyamat (3.28)chandra tara vyuha jnanam (3.29) dhurve tad gati jnanam

(3.27) An absorbed connection with the sun gives you knowledge about the structure of the universe; (3.28) [an absorbed connection] with the moon lets you learn about the stars; (3.29) and [an absorbed connection] with the pole star lets you learn about the movement of the stars.

These sutras are probably allegorical. The sun and the moon are well known aspects in yoga. The word Hatha means sun(Ha) and moon(Tha).

Hatha yoga is the yoga of asana, pranayama and meditation. It is the yoga of the body.

Sun and moon represent the body. The prana, as it comes into the body, travels down two main nadis called Ida and Pingala. The nadis are the energetic channels through which the prana travels in the body. Ida is the moon nadi(starting on the left nostril) and Pingala is the sun nadi(right nostril). Both these nadis end at the pelvic floor. If prana flows through one of these nadis much more than through the other one, our body will be out of balance. One of the points of Hatha yoga is to balance the flow of prana through these main nadis.

This balancing helps to unravel the Kundalini energy. This energy is wound up at the bottom of the pelvic floor, just where Ida and Pingala end. When the Kundalini is awakened it lets the prana go through and the flow from Ida and Pingala connect. Then it travels up the spine, through a third important nadi called Sushumna. This is also what pranayama refers to regarding the releasing of prana (sutra 2.49).

When Kundalini is awakened, prana travels up the spine shining first like fire but then like a million suns and then like a million moons. As the energy travels up, it moves through the chakras. Chakras are the energetic centers of the body that deal with its different functions. The higher the chakra the more spiritual is its purpose. The Kundalini travels from the base chakra(Muladhara) which deals with survival and health of the body all the way up to the crown chakra(Sahaswara) which deals with spiritual enlightenment. The pole star in the sutra may represent the Kundalini energy or one of the chakras.

The sun represents the male or father figure. The father aspect provides structure, boundaries, a universal sense of right and wrong, moral and ethical values. An absorbed connection with the sun will help us tap into this masculine principle which brings structure to the universe.

The moon represents the female or mother figure. The mother provides nurturing, being on our side no matter how wrong we may be, providing a safe place we can always go back to, giving us protection from the world so we can pursue our dreams. An absorbed connection to the moon will allow us to connect to the mystic side of the universe.

(3.30) nabhi chakra kaya vyuha jnanam (3.31) kantha kupe ksut pipasa nivrittih

(3.30) An absorbed connection with the navel chakra teaches you the physiology of the body (3.31) and [an absorbed connection] with the throat chakra lets you get rid of hunger and thirst.

The navel chakra is the second chakra and it is called Svadhisthana. It deals with our reproduction and creative functions. The throat chakra is the fifth, called Vishuddha, and deals with communication and self expression. These two functions are two of the karma-indriyas mentioned in sutra 2.54.

At this stage in the evolutionary paths we are finally learning about ourselves and our true nature, represented by the physiology of the body. The hunger and thirst at this stage of evolution would be more related to spiritual hunger than physical hunger. The throat chakra is related to communication. This communication or connection to other beings is what is going to calm our hunger and thirst.

(3.32) kurma nadyam sthairyam

(3.32) An absorbed connection with the turtle channel gives you poise.

Poise represents being masters of ourselves. Finally we have learned to deal with this world, the physical reality and we have ended our hunger and thirst. We can rest.

The turtle channel is another nadi in the body through which prana moves. It is said to be located inside the chest around the top of the sternum. The Kurma nadi meditation is supposed to bring peace and tranquility.

(3.33) murdha jyotisi siddha darshanam

(3.33) An absorbed connection with the light on the top of the head lets you learn about the masters.

The top of the head is where the seventh chakra is located, the Sahaswara. This chakra is associated with enlightenment. Interestingly this chakra has an inward flow. The sixth chakra – the third eye or Ajna – located on the forehead is the one that projects outwards. This is why we bow our heads in sign of respect, accepting through our seventh chakra what the other person projects out through the sixth.

The masters represent true knowledge. This concept is comparable to sutra 1.50 where true beliefs prevented us from getting false ones. This happens when we are getting close to samadhi.

(3.34) pratibhad va sarvam

(3.34) Or all of these can come at once, in a flash of intuition.

This is the "a-ha" moment. There are two theories on how enlightenment can be achieved. The first one is evolution, the second is realization. In the evolutionary path truth comes in little by little and we see a bit more as we keep opening our eyes progressively. In the realization path we see all at once.

This flash of enlightenment appears in Naropa's story. Naropa was a Brahmin – a scholar in the traditional Indian cast system – who lived in the 10th century A.D. After trying some black magic he found himself in trouble so he searched for a guru, Tilopa, to avoid the consequences. Tilopa made him go through really nasty tests and got him beaten up multiple times. After each test Tilopa told Naropa how bad of a teacher he was and to consider leaving him but Naropa never left. One day while they were sitting by the fire, Tilopa took his shoe off and slapped Naropa on the face. After seeing the stars he understood, as in a flash, the entire Buddhist doctrine. As Naropa's story shows, both paths require the work up front. The difference is in how the awakening comes, either in small chunks or as a onetime payment.

This flash represents enlightenment, we are in the light, or we understand the light. The 'a-ha' moment refers to seeing something or getting it. At this point we are not connected yet. That is samadhi and it comes later.

(3.35) hirdaye chitta samvit

(3.35) An absorbed connection with the heart teaches you about the nature of your own mind.

This is the first samyama exercise of the second section. The first section walked us through the evolutionary path up to enlightenment while this second section has to do with achieving samadhi. As mentioned before, yoga is a process of undoing. This next set of absorbed connection practices remove what makes up our personal reality bit by bit. This sutra represents our view on the world, our beliefs and ideas. That is the first thing we are dropping.

Chitta, or citta or chitt or citt, is a complicated word to interpret. Usually we can find it translated as "mind-stuff" or something similar. Chitta implies consciousness though. It is the part of the mind that expresses consciousness. It is interesting that by practicing samyama on the heart we can understand the true nature of our own mind.

(3.36) sattva purusayoh atyanta asankirnayoh pratyaya avishesah bhogah pararthatvat svartha samyamat purusha-jnanam (3.37) tatah pratibha sravana vedana adarsha asvada varta jayanta (3.38) te samadhau upasargah vyutthane siddhayah

(3.36) The expression of an object and the consciousness that enables it to exist are so intimately intertwined that we believe the object can exist without the consciousness behind it. An absorbed connection with the consciousness that allows reality to express itself through our senses teaches you about that consciousness. (3.37) And from the understanding of this consciousness you can develop higher or transcendental senses. (3.38) However, all these extraordinary abilities – siddhis – are actually obstacles to attaining samadhi.

"Sattva-purusha" appears on several sutras in this chapter. As discussed before, purusha is the universal consciousness. Sattva is the individual expression of an object. It is more than the principle or the idea representing the object. It is its full expression in this reality. But everything we see is an expression of the universal consciousness. All objects are being expressed in reality because of purusha, as purusha is expressing itself through the object. This is the idea that makes everything sacred in yoga philosophy. Everything is an expression of purusha, therefore everything is sacred.

This absorbed connection exercise delves into how reality is expressed by focusing on how we grasp the consciousness through our senses. In yoga philosophy, purusha is pure consciousness and cannot express by itself. This is where prakriti comes in. Prakriti is the universal goo that contains everything. It is pure energy and the basis of everything that exists, no matter how subtle it is. Mind, emotions, gods, ideas or principles are all made of prakriti. Prakriti goes through a process of densification until it becomes a physical object. But the physical object is still made of prakriti in its most inner nature. Purusha animates prakriti. The universal consciousness animates the universal energy. That is how purusha can express itself. The universe is ultimately universal consciousness, purusha, expressing itself through universal energy, prakriti.

This second samyama exercise of the second set represents the reality we are grasping through our senses and our interaction with it. The sutras even tell us to ignore the siddhis acquired in the process of undoing ourselves. This is the next thing we are dropping in our way to samadhi.

These senses or powers, as special as they may be, will prevent us from achieving samadhi unless we let them go. As mentioned in the beginning of the chapter, the last three practices which constitute samyama, while being internal compared to the first five limbs, are external compared to samadhi. The state of samadhi is state of total union and oneness so anything will get in the way.

(3.39) bandha karana shaithilyat prachara samvedanat cha chittasya para sharira aveshah

(3.39) As you understand the reasons for physical reality to exist and understand how consciousness comes into the body, the association between mind and body becomes less fixed. They are then able to decouple and you can enter other bodies.

We are identified with our body and that help us determine who we think we are. In this sutra we are releasing our identification to our own body and gaining the realization that we are everything we see represented by our ability to enter other bodies. We now stop getting our sense of identity from having a body. The process of undoing continues.

(3.40) udana jayat jala panka kantaka adisu asangah utkrantih cha
(3.41) samana jayat jvalanam

(3.40) When you understand the upward flow of prana in your body, you can achieve levitation. (3.41) When you master the flow of prana in the navel area, you become full of life and power.

This sutra moves into a more subtle subject, prana. Prana is the vital energy that regulates and directs our bodies and physical reality. It is the subtlest expression in the physical universe. It is its energy, its driving force. Controlling prana would allow us to command our bodies to levitate or revitalize.

As discussed in sutra 2.50, the vayus are currents of prana in the body. The vayu related with the exhalation during breathing is the Udana vayu which is mentioned in this sutra. This vayu however is not considered to be as important for the movement of prana in the body as the prana or apana vayus.

In the west, Wilhelm Reich introduced the term orgone energy during the 1930s. This orgone energy is described as a universal life force we all hold in our bodies. This is the closest we have come to prana in the west.

(3.42) shrotra akashayoh sambandha samyamat divyam shrotram
(3.43) kaya akashayoh sambandha samyamat laghu tula samatatti cha

(3.42) An absorbed connection with the relationship between hearing and the ether gives you extrasensory hearing, (3.43) and [an absorbed connection] with the relationship between the body and ether, as well as on the lightness of cotton, lets you teleport your body.

From prana, the sutras move into an even more subtle subject, ether. Ether is the basis of everything in the physical universe, even prana. Ether provides the vehicle for prana to express itself. Ether is the building block, prana is the driving energy.

Ether had been in the West since the time of Aristotle up to the end of the 19th century when experiments refuted its existence. Curiously enough, one of the most gifted inventors of all times, Nicola Tesla, was associated with ether (or aether) once again in the 20th century.

As discussed in sutra 3.14 regarding the nature of time, aether would be the material that the 3D film is made of. Both matter and space materialize as they blink from this aether. Aether is the all encompassing goo in which physical reality happens.

When reading the Upanishads, aether is called akasha and it refers to space. The sage Yajnavalkya, who is so popular in the Upanishads, is questioned about the nature of reality and he explains how space is what separates objects. This space, or akasha, is the source of the akashic records, the compendium of all that has happened in the universe. This would make sense according to the sutras concept of time. Akasha, aether, the material of the 3D film of time which holds the past is keeping a record of everything that has happened. Or that may have happened.

Regarding the process of release or undoing ourselves on the way to samadhi, the last two sets of practices release both prana and ether. The level of subtlety keeps increasing as we keep releasing finer aspects of ourselves.

(3.44) bahih akalpita vrittih maha-videha tatah prakasha avarana ksayah,

(3.44) When you realize that everything you see is you, not something outside yourself, you can de-identify from your body. An absorbed connection with this concept lets you understand your spiritual being.

This exercise is the final release of us as a single being, totally de-identifying from the body. Instead of perceiving ourselves as a body moving around, we now realize we are seeing our minds. The body is just a point of reference from which we are looking, but nothing more.

The most subtle vehicle purusha has is the spirit, the grossest one the physical body. Spirit, mind, emotions and ego allow consciousness to experience physical reality through the body. This absorbed connection exercise asks us to change our point of view and instead of thinking ourselves in the world, to think the world to be in our minds. To realize that what we see is our mind at all times. This change of perspective allows us to understand our spiritual self.

Tibetan tradition has an interesting exercise regarding where consciousness is in the body. We are used to seeing the world with our eyes and therefore perceive our consciousness to be in the head. From here the neck, chest, belly and legs are all below, while the top of the head is above. The exercise consists in perceiving our bodies from a different part of the body. If we move our consciousness to our stomach, then we will perceive the chest to be above us. It is easier to start slow and with the eyes closed to get results. Don't try to move your consciousness to the big toe at first but just to the neck. As you get more proficient you can get further away from the head.

(3.45) sthula svarupa suksma anvaya arthavattva samyamad bhuta-jayah (3.46) tatah anima adi pradurbhavah kaya sampad tad dharma anabhighata cha (3.47) rupa lavanya bala vajra samhanana kaya-sampat

(3.45) An absorbed connection with the realization that objects are the result of the interaction of the primordial elements lets you master these elements. (3.46) Through the mastery of the elements, you can make your body perfect, small at will, indestructible, and bring about other exceptional characteristics.(3.47) This perfection includes beauty, grace, strength and the resistance of a diamond.

This absorbed connection exercise takes a more impersonal perspective. It is not a part of ourselves we are connecting to or releasing anymore, but the primordial elements, the bhutas. The purpose of the bhutas is to create physical reality.

The primordial elements – or bhutas – are aether, fire, water, air and earth. Their purpose is to transform aether into earth so physical reality can occur. Aether, or akasha, is the primordial substance from which reality originates as discussed in sutra 3.42. Fire, or tejas, originates from aether. It represents the will, the intention to create. Water, or apas, also originates from aether. It is emotion, the passion to create. Fire and water need to combine to manifest earth but their combination requires balance which is accomplished with the help of air, or vayu, the fourth element. Air represents the mind.

Earth, or prithvi, is the combination of all the others. It is both the coarser and the most sophisticated element. All the other elements are expressed in earth, even aether or space. At the same time earth compliments aether. If we looked at the sky and we saw no stars we would not know how large space was, but by having a physical object out there we can tell how much space there really is. This is how earth compliments aether or space, by giving it context.

The elements are present everywhere, even in everyday life. When we are about to start a new enterprise we start from potential, which is in aether. First we need the idea and the will to start, which is fire. We then need passion to carry our enterprise through, which is water. But all this can only happen if the plan makes sense, if it is balanced, something that is accomplished through the mind, which is air. The realization of our goals represents earth.

The American Indians offer a beautiful explanation on how the elements relate to the races on earth. They see us all as brothers and believe that each race is meant to play a role as we live together. The white race is related to fire or will. The black race is related to water or the body. The yellow race is related to air or mind, and finally the red race is related to earth or emotions and belonging. When looking at the races from this perspective we can see how the white race was the one who created the printing press or the industrial revolution. We can see the deep connection that the black race has to the body, expressed through dance and movement. The yellow race – Tibet – teaches us how everything is mind, and yoga explains how mind and breath are two fishes that swim together. Finally, we see the connection that American Indians have to the land. In their view we belong to earth and not the other way around.

(3.48) grahana svarupa asmita anvaya arthavattva samyamad indriya jayah (3.49) tatah mano-javitvam virarana-bhavah pradhaua jayah

(3.48) An absorbed connection with the senses (indriyas), their processes, nature, relationship to each other and their purpose lets you understand them and how they function. (3.49) With the mastery over the senses you can perceive and interact with the world without using the physical instruments in the body.

Indriyas (sutra 2.54) should be understood as processes in the context of this sutra. Up to now, our process of undoing described in the samyama exercises has covered our physical and spiritual self, prana and the primordial elements. Processes are even more abstract than aether so the sutras progress here into even more subtle territory.

(3.50) sattva purusha anyata khyati matrasya sarva-bhava adhisthatrittvam sarvajnatritvam cha

(3.50) Through the understanding of the difference between the object and the consciousness that makes that object possible, comes omniscience and omnipotence.

These last siddhis are omniscience and omnipotence. They represent the all. As mentioned in sutra 1.51, we need to drop everything in order to achieve samadhi. Our construct of the entire creation is dropped leaving pure consciousness, which is how true connection occurs.

(3.51) tad vairagya api dosa bija ksaya kaivalyam

(3.51) If you can free yourself from these achievements, you can attain absolute freedom.

This sutra is the one that provides the clue regarding the process of undoing that we have been covering from sutra 3.35 to now. The samyama practices and their achievements presented what we needed to drop to attain liberation. And with total liberation comes samadhi.

(3.52) sthani upanimantrane sanga smaya akaranam punuh anista prasangat

(3.52) Don't be proud of your achievements even when being recognized by those you look up to since you may take a step back in your spiritual path.

This is one of the nine obstacles in sutra 1.30: failing to keep the superior perspective once attained. Pride would make us look at what we have obtained with a different perspective than the one we needed to get there. We must keep cultivating the new perspective in order to keep it.

This is a lesson for anything we have achieved in life, whether it is position, skill or relationship. It was our hard work and careful decisions that got us what we wanted. We cannot change our attitude or we will lose what we accomplished. We must keep working and feeding what we have if we want to keep enjoying it. This applies to a company, a marriage or a path to enlightenment.

(3.53) ksana tat kramayoh samyamat viveka-jam jnanam **(3.54)** jati laksana desha anyata anavachchhedat tulyayoh tatah pratipattih(3.55) tarakam sarva visayam sarvatha visayam akramam cha iti viveka jam jnanam

(3.53) Finally, an absorbed connection with the succession of infinitesimal continuous moments, which is time, gives you intuitive knowledge (3.54) and with this knowledge you understand how everything is unique and unrepeatable. (3.55) Also, you become able to transcend time and space and understand the whole of creation, everywhere and everywhen.

And right before the last sutra in the chapter, we go back to the beginning, to an absorbed connection with the nature of time. The first samyama practice, sutra 3.14, worked with time and so this sutra closes the cycle reminding us of the cyclical nature of the universe.

The entire universe is created and destroyed in the day and night of Brahma, to be created and destroyed again, over and over and over. Transcending this cycle is transcending time and the 3D film that we call reality. Sutra 1.19 mentions that looking at life from a superior perspective is how things look when you are dead. This is how it looks when you are beyond time and space, or how it looks when all beliefs are dropped (sutra 1.51) and samadhi is attained.

(3.56) sattva purusayoh suddhi samye kaivalyam iti

(3.56) Once you realize the holiness of everything you see, you can attain total liberation.

Total liberation represents samadhi. We must let everything go if we want to connect to something or someone. Specially we need to release all judgment and all beliefs, so we can connect via who we are. In sutra 3.50 we released all, so samadhi became possible. Now, with the achievement of samadhi comes a realization that everything is sacred, or with the realization that everything is sacred comes samadhi.

Everything being holy means that everything is equal. It was our mind who judged and qualified something as vulgar and something else as sacred. In reality everything is the same, and the differentiation came from us judging.

Our journey started on sutra 3.14, before time, before we come to this reality for the first time. In the beginning we have to get acquainted with physical reality and we get better at living incarnation after incarnation. After we learn how to deal with our lives, we realize there are people around us and we start bringing them into the equation. Our next phase is to realize that we are more than our physical bodies and grow an interest in the mystical. That leads us for the first time to work on ourselves, our true selves, and we start focusing on our spiritual development.

As we grow as universal beings, the task gets more complicated so we need be strong and consistent. We need to keep an eye on the final goal, our enlightenment, as we learn more about our true nature. Eventually we accumulate enough knowledge and wisdom that we become enlightened.

But to achieve samadhi we must let go of everything that is not us. Part by part, all the pieces that create our personal reality must be dropped so we can connect. Once all is dropped, connection to all is possible. Ultimate freedom, freedom from all, is required to connect to all thereby achieving samadhi.

End of the Commentaries to Book 3

Book 4: The Way to Liberation (Kaivalya Pada)

Interpretation of Book 4

(4.1) Siddhis can be obtained through birth, herbs, mantras, austerity or samadhi. (4.2) Evolution occurs by excelling at the phase where we currently are. (4.3) This is not obtained by adding, but by removing extraneous things and letting our true nature flourish, like a gardener helps a tree reach its full potential.

(4.4) The ego allows consciousness to feel singled out, giving us our sense of individuality. (4.5) As a single identity, consciousness goes through multiple incarnations, (4.6) until you break the cycle of incarnations through meditation.

(4.7) The actions of a yogi are neither white nor black. They are what they are. It is others who judge them as good, bad or something in between. (4.8) This judging creates beliefs that will be expressed and reinforced when comparable situations occur. (4.9) These beliefs create karma and you carry them from incarnation to incarnation, regardless of where or when you are born. (4.10) Karma has always existed and it will stick with you unless you do something about it. (4.11) Once you get rid of the source of the karma, it goes away. This source can be a false belief, a wrong motive or an incorrect assumption.

(4.12) The past and the future exist now just like the present does. The nature of the three areas of time are different but the three exist right now, each in their own way. (4.13) Although different, they are based on the same principles – or gunas – and the interaction of these gunas is what gives each area of time its nature. The present is coarser so we perceive it, while past and future are more subtle and they are unavailable to our physical senses.

(4.14) The primordial substance is transformed, creating each unique object. However, the most intimate nature of everything is the same. (4.15) Everything is neutral, the same. It is our personal minds – perceptions, preferences, prejudices or expectations – that make them different. (4.16) But the object does not depend on those perceptions to exist. The object exists independent of the mind observing it. (4.17) We can only understand – or perceive – objects that are in tune with us.

(4.18) The universal consciousness is always aware of all the activities of the personal consciousness, (4.19) but the universal consciousness cannot perceive itself through the personal consciousness. (4.20) Nor can both universal and personal consciousness be perceived at the same time. (4.21) If this could happen, there would be an infinite loop of one consciousness being perceived through the other and the result would be utter confusion.

(4.22) When you look at yourself from the point of view of the universal consciousness you understand who you are. (4.23) Your personal consciousness can look at objects in your reality, at the universal consciousness, and at itself from the point of view of the universal consciousness, thereby fulfilling all its purposes.

(4.24) Although pulled in many directions, the personal consciousness exists for the purpose of the universal consciousness to know itself through an individual point of view. (4.25) Once you realize that you are a single point of universal consciousness looking at the all, the sense of individuality ceases (4.26) and the personal consciousness becomes free. (4.27) The personal consciousness may temporarily lose this freedom as old beliefs, habits and perspectives come back, (4.28) but these can be removed in the same way we discussed previously.

(4.29) Once you lose the interest even for the highest form of knowledge, a blossoming into samadhi occurs, along with the ability to see things are they are. (4.30) False beliefs and karma end as well, (4.31) and with all the veils removed, there is little left to be known. (4.32) The gunas, with their purpose fulfilled, cease to provide the experience we call life. (4.33) They stop providing all those successive and independent moments we call the flow of time. (4.34) The gunas merge back with the all where they came from. Absolute liberation is achieved or the power of consciousness realized. The End.

End of Interpretation of Book 4

Commentary to Book 4

(4.1) janma osadhi mantra tapah samadhi jah siddhyayah

(4.1) Siddhis can be obtained through birth, herbs, mantras, austerity or samadhi.

This last book opens with the theme that occupied the last two thirds of the previous book: the acquisition of siddhis or superpowers. However, this book follows a different approach from the previous three. Instead of giving direct advice, it explains how the universe works. Sutras take a more impersonal tone as they describe the nature of life, time and consciousness. These teachings can be applied to every area in life. We only need be capable of translating the idea from one context to another.

This fourth book is the most interesting from the perspective of the law of correspondence: as above so below, or as we say nowadays, the holographic nature of the universe. This holographic idea is represented in the Indian tradition by Indras's net of jewels. Indra, who is the leader of the Hindu gods, has a net that stretches indefinitely in all directions encompassing the entire universe. At each node there is a jewel and each jewel reflects all the other jewels in the net. It is as if the entire net was contained in each individual node, the all being contained in each of its parts. This is a metaphor for what we call holography nowadays. A hologram is basically a 3D picture, but it has a very distinctive characteristic. If we divide the hologram in two, we don't get two halves. We get two full pictures. So if we have the hologram of a tree and we cut it in two, we get two trees, each of the pieces of the hologram containing the entire hologram. As above so below.

This first sutra talks about siddhis, superpowers, and tells us that we can get them via birth, herbs, mantras, austerity or samadhi. Being able to acquire siddhis through birth gives us a lesson for everything new we start in life, like a new job for example. It is much easier to negotiate perks and special conditions before joining a new company. Once we become employees we are stuck with the deal we got. When working in a home project, it is easier to think about special details before we start nailing pieces together. When we are stuck in life, it pays to seek advice from someone outside and new, so this person can look at the problem with new eyes. All these are applications of the lesson provided by the idea of acquiring siddhis via birth.

The second way to acquire siddhis is herbs. When thinking about herb induced siddhis, mushrooms or LSD come to mind. But let's now think about the allegories. The body represents a system, like a human system for example. We can make a human system perform extraordinary feats by altering their minds. We have seen this work in various ways, from fanaticism to impossible feats accomplished by sports teams. The herbs, the food of human systems, are ideas. Religion, nationality, tradition or social norms are ideas that human systems live on. If we influence the ideas we can change the group's behavior. Realize also how a small mushroom can make us see crazy stuff after we eat it. Once the human system accepts and embraces an idea, thereby eating it, strange visions can occur.

The next mechanism is mantras. In simple terms, a mantra is a phrase that we repeat over and over as part of a meditation. We usually associate it with Tibet, envisioning a monk in a cave chanting the famous "Om Mani Padme Hum" nonstop. The phrase, when used as a mantra, produces a change in the meditating monk. As an allegory, when we repeat something to ourselves over and over we end up believing it. Combining the mushroom approach with the mantra approach we have what we call television. Television is capable of transforming something outrageous into a known fact by repeating it over and over.

The next way, austerity, refers to training. Once more we think of the Tibetan monks who live in caves and train to acquire special powers. Maybe those who have a special skill from birth acquired it through training in a past life. Maybe what we obtain through training in this life is available to us at the time of birth in our next. We see this principle applied in a professional setting all the time. When we change jobs we use the skills acquired in our previous job, our previous life, for our next position. So we are born into our next position with the skills already acquired in a past life.

Lastly, samadhi, being oneness, connects us to everything, so a siddhi becomes natural. Everything becomes connected to us just like our body is connected to us. As an analogy, our purpose in life is always something we feel deeply connected to. When we find it we usually feel like we are one with it so excelling becomes natural.

(4.2) jatyantara parinamah prakriti apurat (4.3) nimittam aprayojakam prakritinam varana bhedas tu tatah ksetrikavat

(4.2) Evolution occurs by excelling at the phase where we currently are. (4.3) This is not obtained by adding, but by removing

extraneous things and letting our true nature flourish, like a gardener helps a tree reach its full potential.

Evolution is not a continuous line but a path formed like a staircase. As we accumulate knowledge and skills, we advance further through each current level. At some point we reach a tipping point where we have enough to move to the next level and the transition occurs. Evolutionary stages are a deterministic process. Once a certain set of conditions is met we acquire the corresponding state. Once that is achieved we get to enjoy all the benefits of that state.

We see that clearly in our careers. When we get a promotion we get everything that the new position encompasses. Until we get that new position we have none of it. Our evolutionary stage is represented by our perspective. It is the context from which we look at the world. The more refined this perspective, the higher the stage. Given an idea, we either get it or we don't, but once we get it we get it fully. It is all or nothing. We either understand something or we don't. This is what creates the shape of a staircase.

The move to the next step is comparable to having an a-ha moment. It is seeing something from a new angle, a new perspective not available until then. These a-ha moments are very personal. We usually try to explain them to others but they are never as moved as we are. They are either not getting it yet or they got it long ago and they do not feel the exhilaration we are feeling.

The gardener image used in the sutra is a perfect one. The gardener creates the ideal conditions for the tree to grow but the growing is done by the tree. We have physical, mental, emotional and spiritual faculties but these are not us. Through our understanding and attitude we create the conditions for our faculties to take their courses. How well our faculties do depends on the understanding and attitudes we feed them.

(4.4) nirmana chittani asmita matrat

(4.4) The ego allows consciousness to feel singled out, giving us our sense of individuality.

Egoism, selfishness or I-ness are referred as causes for suffering throughout the sutras up to this point. This sutra tells us what the ego is for. In our most internal core we are a singled out point of consciousness who is having a human experience. Our truest nature is closer to pure consciousness, of which we are a point.

In the beginning we are not yet aware of our own self as we have not yet developed our individuality. The ego takes care of this for us. The ego

92

provides us with a sense of individuality, of being a single and separate unit. As we very well know already, this is mostly achieved through fear, loneliness and a sense of separation.

The ego helps us through the process of being born at a universal level. Before we experience the ego we are just another point in the sea of consciousness. After enough lives experiencing tough times we acquire our sense of individuality.

The ego is ideally designed to do this job. Its biggest fear is the fear of not being, of ceasing to exist. Anything that may put its existence at risk the ego will run away from. The mantra of the ego is: exist, exist, exist. And by fulfilling this mantra combined with its nature, we are granted our universal individuality.

In the yoga tradition the ego is ahamkara. The ahamkara is deemed sacred as it plays an essential role. The ahamkara is the "chitt-achitt granthi", the knot(granthi) that ties together the conscious(chitt) and the unconscious(achitt). But the knot works both ways. It prepares consciousness to live in physical reality, the unconscious; but at the same time allows the unconscious to believe itself conscious, which is our identification with the ego. Our self is akin to a car with more than one passenger inside. The car represents our physical body. The passengers are our mental body, emotional body and ego. Whoever screams the most gets to drive the car. Although we believe we are the car, we are actually seated in the back seat. We cannot drive the car ourselves, that is why we have a mind, emotions or ego. We need to take control of them in order to take control of our actions. The goal is not to suppress any of these passengers but to learn how to make them do what we want.

Using the role of the ego as an allegory, we can see how a challenge brings a group of people together. Two people that quarrel will join forces if a third party wants what they are fighting about. Challenge is the pressure that draws the two contenders together into a single group. If we want to bring two people together, all we need to do is threaten something they have in common.

(4.5) pravritti bhede prayojakam chittam ekam anekesam (4.6) tatra dhyana jam anasayam

(4.5) As a single identity, consciousness goes through multiple incarnations, (4.6) until you break the cycle of incarnations through meditation.

Sutra 1.32 already recommends we use meditation to fight the nine obstacles. If meditation is the cure to all nine obstacles, this implies that all the obstacles are mental in nature. Sutra 4.6 goes even further in saying that we can break the cycle of incarnation via meditation as well. We can break the obligation to incarnate by using a mental tool such as meditation. Sutra 3.44 asks us to realize that everything we look at is us, to understand that all we see is our minds, not something outside ourselves. These sutras paint life as a mental experience which occurs more inside of us than we realize.

The sutras define meditation as concentrating on an object to the extent that the rest of the world disappears and in book 3 we find a list of samyama practices. When we meditate on an object we have a chance to grasp the real nature of that object, overriding the ego's view. As we meditate more and more our contact with reality increases making the ego permeable or porous. Once the ego allows for our interaction with reality while maintaining our individuality, there is no need to incarnate any more. Incarnation is still a choice, but as willing and conscious participants, not because we need to define our individuality.

(4.7) karma ashukla akrisnam yoginah trividham itaresam(4.8) tatah tad vipaka anugunanam eva abhivyaktih vasananam (4.9) jati desha kala vyavahitanam api anantaryam smriti samskarayoh eka rupatvat

(4.7) The actions of a yogi are neither white nor black. They are what they are. It is others who judge them as good, bad or something in between. (4.8) This judging creates beliefs that will be expressed and reinforced when comparable situations occur. (4.9) These beliefs create karma and you carry them from incarnation to incarnation, regardless of where or when you are born.

We are truly all yogis, students of life and our job is to explore and experience. We do and in the doing we gather information, accumulate knowledge and gain wisdom. With our lives we explore the possibilities of the universe.

When we judge we cut the flow of information, we prevent ourselves from seeing what is in front of us. That is karma, a piece of the puzzle that we have not figured out, something we have not looked at yet. All we have to do is make it conscious, look at it. Fear or judgment keeps things hidden inside, so we associate karma with fear while the key is in what the fear is hiding beneath. All we have to do is gather enough strength to look at it. Once we look and we make it conscious we free it and karma is released.

In the yoga tradition our life mission is called dharma. This is what we are supposed to do in life and is usually associated with our duty in society.

However, there is a more universal view of dharma. Dharma could also be seen as the mission we signed up for before coming to this world. Our initial mission is defining ourselves, our individuality, but once this is underway, other choices become available. We could explore the body possibilities through dance or gymnastics, the mind through mathematics or finances, or relationships through family or business.

Whatever mission we chose we must explore fully or we would be missing something. If we hide or shut down any part of the mission we create lessons we have not learned yet. This is karma. Dharma is the mission and karma are the remaining areas that we have not yet explored in that dharma.

(4.10) tasam anaditvam cha ashisah nityatvat (4.11) hetu phala ashraya alambana samgrihitatvat esam abhave tad abhavah

(4.10) Karma has always existed and it will stick with you unless you do something about it. (4.11) Once you get rid of the source of the karma, it goes away. This source can be a false belief, a wrong motive or an incorrect assumption.

Fear is an effect not a cause. The cause is the misunderstanding that makes us see something as frightening. Once we understand, fear goes away. Understanding allows us to release the experience we were shutting down underneath the fear thereby integrating the information and releasing the karma in the process.

We could say that in the beginning, before time started, all we had was karma. It was all lessons to be had and experiences to be understood. Then we chose our missions, our dharmas, and we jumped into the time universe. As we lived and learned we progressed, completing our dharma and decreasing our karma. Once the dharma is complete and we have fully understood the topic we wanted to study, there is no more karma left.

Karma and ignorance are intimately related. The things we ignore are the lessons to be had, the karma. Ignorance, avidya, is the core of karma and the root of suffering, as sutra 2.4 says. This is also why sutra 2.15 is usually translated as "life is suffering". No suffering, no ignorance, no karma, no dharma, no lesson to be learned, no need for time and space. Ignorance is the point. Suffering is how we feel about ignorance until we realize that ignorance is the point.

(4.12) atita anagatam svarupatah asti adhva bhedat dharmanam (4.13) te vyakta suksmah guna atmanah

(4.12) The past and the future exist now just like the present does. The nature of the three areas of time are different but the three exist right now, each in their own way. (4.13) Although different, they are based on the same principles – or gunas – and the interaction of these gunas is what gives each area of time its nature. The present is coarser so we perceive it, while past and future are more subtle and they are unavailable to our physical senses.

Gunas are universal principles; they are laws. They affect all at all levels. The first guna is activity(rajas), the second is realization(sattva) and the third is decay(tamas).

First there is movement and with it there is creation. Creation comes from chaos looking for order. The artist gets a flash of inspiration and writes down some quick thoughts; then there is work to get the job done. This activity is driven by the fires of creation and creativity. This is rajas. This is will and passion.

Then the job is done and the work is complete. We enjoy it and it delights our eyes. A sense of satisfaction comes from a job well done and the enjoyment of having that which we created. This is sattva. This is fulfillment.

But as time passes that which once shined becomes dull. Enjoyment ends as we watch what we created lose its appeal. Decay and destruction take over. This is tamas. This is wisdom.

Tamas is the most static and as such is associated with the past. We learn from our pasts. The future is full of opportunity and therefore is associated with rajas. Finally the present, the accomplishment, the realization is associated with sattva.

The cycle of the gunas is the process of life. The more of these cycles we go through in a lifetime, the more intense our life is. The Sanskrit word for happiness is "sukha" – mentioned in sutra 2.42. "Su" means good and "kha" means hole. The word sukha represents a wheel whose hole is in the center thus providing a smooth ride. Happiness is not a fixed state but the ability to smoothly ride the cycle of the gunas, moving gracefully from one guna to the next.

Happiness does not come from preserving a sattvic state since it will invariably decay. Happiness comes from knowing how to live. This is what the Tibetans call "thab" or method: "One who knows how to go about it could live comfortably even in hell." The method requires we act according to the guna that is currently in effect. We should find happiness at work during a rajasic state, happiness after a job well done in a sattvic state, and happiness in the release of the past and the integration of the gained wisdom during a tamasic state.

(4.14) parinama ekatvat vastu tattvam (4.15) vastu samye chitta bhedat tayoh vibhaktah panthah

(4.14) The primordial substance is transformed, creating each unique object. However, the most intimate nature of everything is the same. (4.15) Everything is neutral, the same. It is our personal minds – perceptions, preferences, prejudices or expectations – that make them different.

Primordial matter is prakriti (see sutra 3.36). Prakriti is neither good nor bad, it is energy for lack of a better word. It makes all and supports all. It just behaves according to its laws. If we kick a ball it will roll until it eventually stops. That is prakriti following the universal rules. First we see the law of cause and effect. For every action there is a reaction demonstrated in the ball moving after we kick it. Then there is the law of inertia. The balls keeps moving while friction slows it down until it stops. Judgment appears when we put expectations on how much we would have liked the ball to roll. If we want the ball to keep rolling we will judge the ball stopping as bad. However, the ball is just rolling.

(4.16) na cha eka chitta tantram ched vastu tat pramanakam tada kim syat

(4.16) But the object does not depend on those perceptions to exist. The object exists independent of the mind observing it.

If a tree falls in a forest and there is nobody there to hear it, does it make a sound? The sutras say that the answer is yes. Prakriti follows rules blindly. Purusha is the one looking at what is happening. Prakriti is universal energy. Purusha is universal consciousness.

As we live and learn, we are looking at how life works. We are looking at the laws that rule prakriti. Learning about life is learning about how prakriti behaves. Our emotions, ideas and feelings are part of prakriti. In the yoga tradition prakriti is said to be like a mirror. What prakriti is reflecting is the consciousness looking at it, purusha. The reason purusha is interested in life and how prakriti works is because prakriti is reflecting purusha. Therefore by purusha looking at how prakriti behaves purusha learns about itself.

We can apply this principle to our yoga practice. When we put our body through the challenge of asana we see how it behaves. We observe it. This exercise has value in two ways. First, the body is following the same universal rules that everything else does, so by observing the process in the body we can learn about the processes in the universe. Second, the body is us. It is as healthy, sick, limber, inflexible, strong or weak as we are. The body is our reflection in the physical world, it is our creation. By watching the struggle that the body goes through during our practice, we learn how we work and what we have going on inside.

(4.17) tad uparaga apeksitvat chittasya vastu jnata ajnatam

(4.17) We can only understand – or perceive – objects that are in tune with us.

We see between red and violet. We cannot see infrared or ultraviolet colors. There is a minimum and a maximum frequency beyond which we cannot go with any physical device we create. That is what we can perceive and what we call this reality. We cannot really tell what is beyond those thresholds. There could be entire worlds and universes there that also don't know we are here.

Psychologically, we become friends with people who think like us. We could say that we live in the same wavelength. If we want to understand someone who we don't easily relate to, we have to make an effort. We need to empathize with new acquaintances and try to see life from their perspective, from a different and new wavelength. All parents are forced to do this with their children as they grow up. The world that their children are living in does not always make sense to the parents so they need to empathize with them and try to look at their new world with new eyes.

(4.18) sada jnatah chitta vrittayah tat prabhu purusasya aparinamitvat (4.19) na tat svabhasam drishyatvat (4.20) eka-samaye cha ubhaye anavadharanam (4.21) chitta antara drishye buddhi-buddheh atiprasangah smriti sankarah cha

(4.18) The universal consciousness is always aware of all the activities of the personal consciousness, (4.19) but the universal consciousness cannot perceive itself through the personal consciousness. (4.20) Nor can both universal and personal consciousness be perceived at the same time. (4.21) If this could happen, there would be an infinite loop of one consciousness being perceived through the other and the result would be utter confusion.

We are a point of universal consciousness. If we could see this universal consciousness, since it is us, we would see us looking at us through us looking at us forever. Our personal point of view is to some extent artificial. As we undo ourselves we start seeing from a universal point of view simply because that is our nature. After all, everything is purusha, everything is just consciousness.

As Krishnamurti asked: "Is there anything sacred beyond the mind?" The mind refers to the universe and the word sacred refers to something that is not temporary, as this universe is. There is no way for us to know how this universe happens, as all we have available to explain this universe is this universe. We cannot look at this place from outside. We are actually inside looking at what is inside.

Allegorically this reflects what bad judges we are of ourselves. It is very hard to know how we look through other people's eyes, and most of the time we are wrong. We can infer how we must be from other's behaviors, but we cannot know for certain.

(4.22) chitteh apratisamkramayah tad akara apattau sva buddhi samvedanam (4.23) drastri drisya uparaktam chittam sarva artham

(4.22) When you look at yourself from the point of view of the universal consciousness you understand who you are. (4.23) Your personal consciousness can look at objects in your reality, at the universal consciousness and at itself from the point of view of the universal consciousness, therefore fulfilling all its purposes.

We are a singled out point of consciousness exploring the universe. We are exploring this place, learning about it and in turn about ourselves. But to know everything we need to know all that can be seen as well as ourselves, since it is we who are doing the seeing. We need to know the entire universe – prakriti – our individual mind – chitta – and the universal consciousness – purusha. It is like seeing all that there is to see plus ourselves doing the looking.

We see this principle applied in scientific experiments. An experiment starts from a hypothesis which the experiment is trying to prove. The hypothesis is the perspective, the individual consciousness or point of view from which the experiment will be conducted. The execution of the experiment is prakriti, or reality, the fulfillment of universal laws. Purusha is the foundation of that hypothesis, or the overall theory that both supports and would be proven if the hypothesis is confirmed. The theory and the hypothesis are joined just like our individual consciousness is to purusha. And the experiment and the hypothesis depend on each other just like prakriti and purusha are intertwined as well.

(4.24)tad asankheya vasanabhih chittam api parartham samhatya karitvat **(4.25)** vishesa darshinah atma bhava bhavana vinivrittih **(4.26)**tada viveka nimnam kaivalya pragbharam chittam

(4.24) Although pulled in many directions, the personal consciousness exists for the purpose of the universal consciousness to know itself through an individual point of view. (4.25) Once you realize that you are a single point of universal consciousness looking at the all, the sense of individuality ceases (4.26) and the personal consciousness becomes free.

Kaivalya, liberation, gives the name to the fourth book. Pada means "way" so kaivalya pada can be translated as the way to liberation. Kaivalya also means aloneness, absolute oneness or freedom. Freedom from belief, attachment, the causes of suffering and ignorance.

Once we realize our place in life we become part of it. While we don't know what we are supposed to do we feel like outcasts and like we don't fit anywhere. Once we discover our purpose, destiny and passion we see how we fit within the overall fabric of life. Our passion in life is our purpose which makes our sense of loneliness disappear. At the same time we realize we are unique since nobody else shares our particular purpose. In this sense we are alone in our singularity. Liberation comes when we find our unique role to play in the universe and seeing how that role fits within the whole.

Book 4 introduces a key revelation, hinted at in the previous books, but not explicitly stated until now. We are consciousness. We are an individuated point of consciousness. With this revelation also comes an interesting evolutionary process to obtain our individuality. This process is based on the ego, reincarnation, meditation and our sense of connection.

The process starts in a sea of consciousness. Everything is consciousness. We are a point in it but it is difficult to identify ourselves while swimming in that sea of consciousness. It is like identifying a drop of water in the ocean. We need to remove all the water around that one drop to see the drop. That is our objective.

That is why we jump into the physical realm and we endow ourselves with an ego. The role of the ego is to encapsulate that point of consciousness, separating it from everything else so we can clearly identify it. We are removing all the water around the one drop we are interested in so we can see the drop.

Incarnation after incarnation, we let the ego do its job, allowing the feeling of separation to create an awareness of individuality. As we live, beliefs, fears, memories or experiences get attached to the ego, creating layers. The layers separate us from other people and help us present the persona that we use to live our lives.

Once we have lived enough lives we can start the process of undoing and little by little getting rid of these layers. We need to go beyond the layers to connect at a deeper level. We want to connect from a real place in ourselves to a real place in the other. What we truly are is beyond all the layers, fears, memories and beliefs. As we reach out, we have to go beyond our ego to connect to the reality outside of us. And as we connect to others, we want to go through their layers, connecting to what is real in them. We already have an expression for this. We say "I got through to him".

According to the sutras, meditation is what allows us to get through our layers and connect to what lies beyond our encapsulated selves. As barriers fall, connection becomes possible and once all barriers are gone, Samadhi occurs. We have accomplished the purpose of this physical life, obtaining our individuality. At this point reincarnation is no longer mandatory, but a choice.

(4.27) tachchhidresu pratyaya antarani samskarebhyah (4.28) hanam esam kleshavat uktam

(4.27) The personal consciousness may temporarily lose this freedom as old beliefs, habits and perspectives come back, (4.28) but these can be removed in the same way we discussed previously.

This is mentioned as one of the nine obstacles in sutra 1.30 – failing to keep the superior perspective once attained. Once we attain liberation we do not just fly away. In the yoga tradition, after achieving samadhi we realize the state of jivanmukti. This state is described as a state of oneness while incarnated in the physical universe. The sutras expect us to achieve this perspective while alive. Why would they tell us to work on keeping the superior perspective if not?

In the western tradition we only get to heaven once dead. It seems to conflict with the eastern concept of samadhi if we consider heaven to be a place. If we understand heaven as a perspective, both philosophies can be reconciled. Heaven would correspond to the superior perspective, which is how things look when you are dead as sutra 1.19 says. Once dead, you merge back with the universal consciousness, which feels like heaven.

(4.29) prasankhyane api akusidasya sarvatha viveka khyateh dharma-meghah samadhih

(4.29) Once you lose the interest even for the highest form of knowledge, a blossoming into samadhi occurs, along with the ability to see things are they are.

Here is the difference between thinking you are something and knowing you are something. As we said, we are bad judges of ourselves, so the only way to know who we are must come via realization. It must be a state of being, as samadhi is a state of oneness.

When we accept who we are we don't need anyone's acceptance any more. There is no need for external validation. We are who we are and we accept it. We don't need to convince anybody of anything because we know we are real. Once we accept ourselves, just how we are, we suddenly have a real point of view from which to look. The key is that it is finally real. Until now we had been trying to be someone else, or to fit into what others thought we should be.

What we are may be nice or mean, grateful or ungrateful, sincere or deceitful, but whatever we are we have made peace with it. Once we accept who we are we can look at life and understand it. We can see reality because we are looking from a point of view that is real. We misjudged what we were looking at because we had a false image of ourselves. We don't need supreme knowledge or asceticism to see what is real. We just need to learn and accept who we are.

(4.30) tatah klesha karma nivrittih (4.31) tada sarva avarana mala apetasya jnanasya anantyat jneyam alpam (4.32) tatah kritarthanam parinama krama samaptih gunanam (4.33) ksana pratiyogi parinama aparanta nigrahyah kramah

(4.30) False beliefs and karma end as well, (4.31) and with all the veils removed, there is little left to be known. (4.32) The gunas, with their purpose fulfilled, cease to provide the experience we call life. (4.33) They stop providing all those successive and independent moments we call the flow of time.

At the universal level, once karma is gone, all would be known so there would be no more false beliefs. Everything would be understood. The gunas could stop acting and providing the experience we call life. Time and space would cease. Prakriti stops moving, once purusha has seen it.

If the end of karma marks the end of the universe, the desire to know had to be the reason the universe was created. In the beginning all was unknown, all was karma. That was the cue for the gunas to start acting and creating the experience of space and time.

Therefore, what created the experience of life was purusha's desire to know, to learn and observe. Its desire to have the experience. The entire universe had to be fueled by this desire since once this was fulfilled, the universe ceased. The slippery "I" is sometimes explained as the will to live. This view would be in line with the purusha as wanting to have this experience.

Also, purusha has to impregnate every bit of prakriti. If not, there would be something that would be unknown, a lost perspective or missed experience. Prakriti, as unconscious as it may be, is infused with purusha — totally conscious — as it unfolds and makes life happen.

On a personal level, we are playing the part of purusha as we come to this life with the desire to learn and experiment. Once we understand how this whole game works and see how everything happens, even behind the scenes, we lose interest and we can let go from this physical experience.

(4.34) purusha artha sunyanam gunanam pratiprasavah kaivalyam svarupa pratistha va chiti shaktih iti

(4.34) The gunas merge back with the all where they came from. Absolute liberation is achieved or the power of consciousness realized. The End.

Our process of individualization is complete and the cycle of re-birth broken. The ego has accomplished its purpose and we are a universal entity now. We do not have to incarnate any more unless we choose to. When being born again we experience life the same way as someone who is working on their own individuality, but we can return to this liberated perspective more easily.

As sutra 1.1 says, this is yoga. All this was yoga. Yoga is the process of life and we are all yogis. We are pure consciousness experiencing a universe that we have created with the purpose of knowing ourselves.

End of the Commentaries to Book 4

Epilogue

What a book eh? Reality is presented as something so rich, so full of information and totally logical, but at the same time mysterious and appealing.

The yoga sutras' approach is pure alchemy. They make philosophy real, and by real I mean physical. First there is a use of physical reality to gain knowledge in the form of asana, pranayama and meditation. It is as if we could squeeze the body for knowledge as we would do with an orange for juice. By putting the body into difficult situations – asanas – we can observe the way it reacts, and in the observation gain knowledge. When the knowledge is put in a universal perspective we gain wisdom. This is the way up, described in the first two books.

Then, there is the way down. This wisdom is tested against the reality of the physical realm. Only this can confirm whether we have truly understood the theory or not. The samyama practices are tests that make clear to us whether we truly understood anything and we have enough control over our body – or bodies.

But there is a very practical and positive side to philosophy. By having a larger perspective of life, our daily stuff seems smaller and we feel we can deal with it. This higher view will help us get through the tough stuff in life and enjoy it a bit more.

Take care,

Moises

Glossary

Ahimsa: non violence. One of the yamas.

Apana vayu: the current of prana in the body (vayu) related to eliminating.

Asana: yoga posture.

Dharana: one of the eight limbs of yoga. Concentration.

Dhyana: one of the eight limbs of yoga. Meditation.

Guna: universal principle determining the flow of life. Stage in the lifecycle of any being.

Indriya: the senses in yoga literature. There are five senses to take the world in and other five to act on the world.

Ishvara-pranidhana: surrendering to a higher power.

Kriya Yoga: yoga in action.

Maya: illusion. It refers to physical reality being an illusion.

Nadi: channel through which prana flows in the body.

Niyama: one of the eight limbs of yoga. Observances to follow.

Prakriti: universal substance. The substance which makes all that can be known.

Prana: universal energy.

Prana vayu: the current of prana in the body (vayu) related to inhaling.

Pranayama: one of the eight limbs of yoga. Control of the flow of prana in the body through the breath.

Pratyahara: one of the eight limbs of yoga. Withdrawal from the senses.

Purusha: universal consciousness.

Samadhi: oneness, a state of connection to all. Also one of the eight limbs of yoga.

Samyama: absorbed connection. Combination of dharana (concentration), dhyana (meditation) and Samadhi (oneness).

Siddhi: extraordinary ability.

Sutra: a rule or aphorism in Sanskrit literature.

Vayu: the Air element. Also a current of prana in the body.

Yama: one of the eight limbs of yoga. Observances to avoid.

Bibliography

These are the translations and interpretations of The Yoga Sutras of Patanjali that I used for this book:

- Swami Venkatesananda
- Swami Jnaneshvara Bharati
- Chip Hartranft
- Yogi Madhvācārya / Michael Beloved
- Geshe Michael Roach & Christie McNally
- Alex Bailey
- Alice Bailey